THE DIARY O
WORKING MAN

1872–1873

BILL WILLIAMS

in the

Forest of Dean

Other titles by Ralph Anstis:

The Story of Parkend, a Forest of Dean Village

Warren James and the Dean Forest Riots

The Industrial Teagues and the Forest of Dean

Around the Forest

Dean Forest Stories

THE DIARY OF A WORKING MAN

1872–1873

BILL WILLIAMS

in the

Forest of Dean

EDITED BY BESS AND RALPH ANSTIS

ALAN SUTTON PUBLISHING LIMITED

First published in the United Kingdom in 1994
Alan Sutton Publishing Limited
Phoenix Mill · Far Thrupp · Stroud · Gloucestershire

Published in the United States of America in 1994
Alan Sutton Publishing Inc
83 Washington Street · Dover · NH 03820

British Library Cataloguing in Publication Data

A catalogue record for this book is available from the British Library.

ISBN 0-7509-0584-0

Library of Congress Cataloging in Publication Data
Williams, Bill, 1847–
Diary of a working man: Bill Williams, Forest of Dean, 1872–1873
edited by Bess and Ralph Anstis.
ISBN 0-7509-0584-0
1. Dean, Forest of (England) – Social life and customs. 2. Working class – England – Dean, Forest of – History – 19th century. 3. Working class – England – Dean, Forest of – Diaries. 4. Williams, Bill, 1847–Diaries, I. Anstis, Bess, 1922– . II. Anstis, Ralph. III. Title
DA670.D25W55 1994
942.4' 13 –dc20 94-1791
CIP

Typeset in 10/15 Garamond.
Typesetting and origination by
Alan Sutton Publishing Limited
Printed and bound in Great Britain by
Ebenezer Baylis, Worcester.

To all the men who worked
at Trafalgar Colliery

Contents

Acknowledgements

We are grateful to Gregory Jones, the owner of the diary, for permission to publish it. For information in the Introduction, Notes and Appendix, thanks are owed to Les Tuffley, Jack Aston, who now occupies Trafalgar House, and Clive Brain, the great-grandson of Jim Brain, the bailiff mentioned in the diary. We are especially indebted to Dave Tuffley for providing many facts, reading the typescript and making valuable suggestions. Our thanks also go to the following authors:

Anon, *Souvenir History of the Baptist Church, Cinderford.* Cinderford, 1910.

Thomas Bright, *The Rise of Non-Conformity in the Forest of Dean.* Forest of Dean Local History Society, Coleford, 1954.

Cyril Hart, *The Industrial History of Dean.* David & Charles, Newton Abbot, 1971.

Timothy Mountjoy, *Sixty-two Years in the Life of a Forest of Dean Collier* or *The Life, Labours and Deliverances of a Forest of Dean Collier.* A Chilver, London and Coventry, 1887.

Ian Pope, *Cinderford's 'Pony Express' Mail Delivery.* Article in *The Forester,* 19 March 1993.

Ian Pope, Bob Haw and Paul Kerau, *Severn & Wye Railway* Volume 2. Wild Swan Publications Ltd, Upper Bucklebury, Berks, 1985.

David Verey, *The Buildings of England. Gloucestershire: the Vale and the Forest of Dean.* Penguin Books, 1980.

We thank the owners of the photographs reproduced: Jack Aston, Maurice Bent, Cyril Hart, Barbara Griffith, Cynthia Jack, Elsie Olivey, Alec Pope, Ian Pope, Brinley Rodway, Foxdell

Carriages and the Sidmouth Donkey Sanctuary; and Audrey Benjamin for permission to reproduce the picture of Euroclydon.

We also thank Bath University, the Church of Jesus Christ of Latter Day Saints of Cheltenham and Coalway, the public libraries at Newport and Hereford, the Record Offices at Cwmbran, West Glamorgan, Gloucester and Kew, the Registrars of Births and Deaths at Lydney, Ross-on-Wye and Pontypool, the staff of the Gloucestershire Collection at Gloucester Library, the New Zealand Society of Genealogists and the New Zealand National Archives Office.

The design of the birth certificate on page xiv is Crown copyright and is reproduced with the permission of the Controller of HMSO.

Editors' Note

Parts of the diary have been difficult to transcribe: some sections were written in pencil and have faded with the years; the ink in others has also faded; a little of the shorthand is indecipherable; and a few words under young Gregory Jones's crayonning have proved difficult to read. Text that is illegible has been indicated.

The text has been lightly edited. Capital letters have been inserted and removed as appropriate, abbreviations have been expanded for clarity and the erratic punctuation has been altered to make the text easier to read. Words added in explanation have been put in square brackets. A series of dots indicates where, in a few places, we have cut the text. The original spelling has been left uncorrected.

Bill's world while writing the diary.

Introduction

Bill Williams was twenty-five when he decided to keep a diary. Short though it is – he kept it for less than a year – it gives an intriguing insight into the life of a young, unmarried man who lived in a small industrial town in west Gloucestershire's Forest of Dean in the 1870s. It shows the pattern of his work days and his Sundays, how he spent his money and what he did in his spare time.

Part of the interest of Bill Williams's diary is that he was an educated working-class man. At a time when probably almost half of working people were unable to read and write he had, by a strange conjunction of events, become quite well educated and was able to set down confidently on paper his observations on life and people. He did this with a charm and insight that endear him to us 120 years later.

The diary was discovered in 1965 by its present owner, Gregory Jones, when he was five years old. He found it, thick with dust, in an old trunk in a wooden shed in a field near his house at Cinderford in the Forest of Dean. Mr Jones recalls that there were other books in the trunk, but his impression is that they were all printed books. Young Gregory used the diary to scribble in, but his aunt, realizing its value, took it away from him. Thus it was preserved for us. We can only wring our hands at the thought of the other treasures in the trunk that must have been destroyed, but we can console ourselves with the gem that young Gregory retrieved.

Bill Williams was born on 7 March 1847 in the parish of Trelleck, a few miles south of Monmouth in Gwent. He was illegitimate. His mother, Elizabeth Williams, an illiterate country girl, had in her teens gone to work as a servant at Lydart

CJ 329141

B. Cert.
S.R.

CERTIFIED COPY of an ENTRY OF BIRTH
COPI DILYS O GOFNOD GENEDIGAETH

Pursuant to the Births and Deaths Registration Act 1953

Registration District / Dosbarth Cofrestru: Monmouth

1847 BIRTH in the Sub-district of / GENEDIGAETH yn Is-ddosbarth: Trelleck in the / yn County of Monmouth

Columns:— / Colofnau:— No. / Rhif	1 When and where born / Pryd a lle y ganwyd	2 Name, if any / Enw os oes un	3 Sex / Rhyw	4 Name, and surname of father / Enw a chyfenw'r tad	5 Name, surname, and maiden surname of mother / Enw, cyfenw a chyfenw morwynol y fam	6 Occupation of father / Gwaith y tad	7 Signature, description, and residence of informant / Llofnod, disgrifiad a chyfeiriad yr hysbysydd	8 When registered / Pryd y cofrestrwyd	9 Signature of registrar / Llofnod y cofrestrydd	10* Name entered after registration / Enw a gofnodwyd wedi'r cofrestru
269	Seventh of March 1847 in the Parish of Trelleck	William Henry	Boy	—	Elizabeth WILLIAMS	—	The x mark of Elizabeth Williams Mother Trelleck	Twelfth of April 1847	William Miller Registrar	—

Cofrestrydd

*See note overleaf *Gweler drosodd

I, / Yr wyf i, Nancy Bennett Deputy Superintendent Registrar for the District of / Cofrestrydd Arolygol Dosbarth Pontypool in the / yn County of Gwent

do hereby certify that this is a true copy of the entry No. / yn tystio yma fod hyn yn gopi cywir o gofnod Rhif 269 in the Register of Births No. / yng Nghofrestr Genedigaethau Rhif 3 for the above-named Sub-district, and that such Register is now legally in my custody. / yr Is-ddosbarth a enwyd uchod, ac a gedwir yn gyfreithlon gennyf i.

Witness my hand this / Tyst wfy o'r hyn sydd dan fy llaw y 5th day of / dydd o fis June 1992

Nancy Bennett Deputy Superintendent Registrar / Cofrestrydd Arolygol

CAUTION:—It is an offence to falsify a certificate or to make or knowingly use a false certificate or a copy of a false certificate intending it to be accepted as genuine to the prejudice of any person, or to possess a certificate knowing it to be false without lawful authority.

RHYBUDD:—Y mae'n drosedd ffugio tystysgrif neu gwneud neu'n fwriadol i ddefnyddio tystysgrif ffug neu copi o dystysgrif ffug gan fwriadu iddi gael ei derbyn fel un ddilys gan ragfarnu unrhyw berson, neu i fod yn berchen tystysgrif gan wybod ei bod yn ffug heb ganiatâd cyfreithlon.

Printed by authority of the Registrar General / Argraffwyd dan awdurdod y Cofrestrydd Cyffredinol

Bill Williams's birth certificate.

House, a large country house at Mitchel Troy near Monmouth. There she worked for Thomas Oakley JP and his family.

The Oakleys were well-to-do. Attached to the house they had a farm of over 600 acres, which no doubt was profitably run. Their wealth was shown by the retinue of seven living-in servants, which included a footman, as well as outdoor staff. The eldest son of the family was a solicitor who practised in Monmouth. Another was a curate and a third was also to become a clergyman.

Elizabeth Williams was seduced by the eldest son, Thomas William Oakley, who was then unmarried and about twenty-nine or thirty years old. She became pregnant, and when her pregnancy was too great to conceal she went to Trelleck, where her baby was born. The child was christened William Henry Williams in the parish church ten days later.

Oakley's seduction of Elizabeth was perhaps just another example of the son of a Victorian squire taking advantage of a working girl, but he did not deny his paternity; he accepted responsibility and maintained his son for many years. Oakley married a few years after Bill's birth and sired many more children, but he kept in touch with Bill. His address at Lydart House is in the back of the diary, and Bill twice reminds himself that he must write to 'T.W.O.', as he calls him.

What happened to Elizabeth we do not know, and Bill doesn't mention her in his diary. She may have died shortly after his birth: an unmarried Elizabeth Williams died in Penallt near Trelleck in 1849, aged twenty. On the other hand, knowing that Oakley was prepared to pay for her son to be looked after, she may have abandoned him and gone off to start life afresh, for the disgrace of becoming pregnant out of wedlock was considerable in Victorian times, and bringing up an illegitimate child a constant reminder of that disgrace.

In any event the child was soon farmed out to George and Rachel Herbert, an elderly couple who lived in Monnow Street, Monmouth. The 1851 census refers to Bill as George Herbert's nephew, but the Herberts were more likely to have been paid child-minders. Oakley paid for the cost of Bill's stay with them and later arranged for his education at William Bradshaw's private school, which was only a few yards down the road from the Herberts' house.

By the time he was fourteen Bill had left the Herberts. It was customary at the time for gentry who accepted responsibility for their illegitimate offspring to make a settlement when the child reached that age; then they could feel that their duty was done. When Bill was about fourteen his father arranged for him to work in the office of a fellow solicitor, Samuel Farmer, whose well-established practice was in Widemarsh Street in the centre of Hereford. Samuel Farmer's son, young Sam, was articled to his father, and he and Bill became friends. Sam qualified as a solicitor and in due course took over his father's practice.

It seems that, while he was with the Farmers, Bill's education expanded. Entries in the diary show that he knew something about music, church art and literature. Also his extensive knowledge of the bible and religion in general are greater than one would expect from anyone who had attended only Mr Bradshaw's establishment. These additions to his education may have resulted from his contact with the Farmer family; or he may have acquired them from the Revd John Williams, who was known to Bill since his address is in the back of the diary. The Revd Williams was a retired widower who lived at Pencraig near Ross-on-Wye with his daughter. It is almost certain that he was no relation of Bill's, for he was born in Northampton and had come to Pencraig from Radnorshire. While at Pencraig he was described as 'a clergyman without care of souls' and, not being encumbered with a flock, he may have tutored Bill. We do not know, though we suspect that Bill's Christian conscience, which so often pricked him in his self-imagined wickedness, must have been honed by a religious man like the Revd Williams.

Sometime in the 1860s Bill left Hereford and, though the reason for his departure cannot be discovered, it ended his education. Whatever that had amounted to – and it was certainly better than the circumstances of his birth augured – and whatever his natural abilities, they had been insufficient to enable him to climb far up the social scale, for we next hear of him in 1868 working in Gloucester. In 1871 he was a porter at Gloucester railway station, then in 1872 he obtained work as a storekeeper and clerk at Trafalgar Colliery in the Forest of Dean. Shortly after his arrival there he began to write his diary.

In the 1870s the Forest of Dean was a strange mixture of verdant beauty and industrial ugliness. Cinderford, where Bill Williams lived, was the biggest town in the Forest. Half a century earlier it had not existed; then the Industrial Revolution had taken off. Deep coal pits were sunk; old iron mines were rejuvenated; and iron works, soon to be spitting flames, smoke and noise, were constructed. In a few decades Cinderford became a town of some eleven thousand souls. With its unmade, rutted roads, its overcrowded houses, its stagnant pools of raw sewage in the streets and its deaths from cholera and typhoid, Cinderford in the 1860s and '70s was the most unhealthy town in Dean, and the only one to compare in squalor with the new towns of the north of England spawned by the Industrial Revolution. A government inspector wrote in an official report in 1869 that he had never seen a town anywhere in a worse sanitary condition than Cinderford.

None of this is reflected in the diary. Indeed, Bill gives the impression that Cinderford was not an unpleasant town to live in. Perhaps he accepted the unhealthy conditions as part of life and not worth commenting on.

Trafalgar Colliery, where Bill worked, was deep in the Forest, a couple of miles from Cinderford. He was in charge of the stores at the pit-head, but he also had other duties at the colliery. He took his turn in booking the colliers in and out of the pit, weighing the coal that they sent to the surface and compiling their work sheets. He also carried out a variety of other jobs, such as writing business letters for the boss and doing shopping for him and his wife in Cinderford, often in the evening in his own time.

Bill's hours were from 6.00 a.m. until about 5.00 p.m. On Saturdays he worked until about 4.00 p.m. Twice a week he also worked a late shift voluntarily because he wanted the money, and on those nights he did not finish until after midnight. Even so he had to be at work first thing the following morning. His work does not seem to have been onerous. He had breakfast and dinner during working hours, and often found time to write his diary and letters to his friends. For his duties during the day he earned about £1 1*s* 6*d* (£1.08) a week. This was the wage many a collier in the pit took home for the expenditure of far more sweat. For working a night shift he received 3*s* 4*d*.

Trafalgar Colliery was owned by William Blanch Brain and his brother, Thomas Bennett Brain. They employed about nine hundred men there. They also owned other collieries and iron mines in the Forest.

William Brain lived with his family at Trafalgar House, which adjoined the pit. He lived in some style, with coach and livery, coachman and crest. He could be said to have 'arrived', for he was only twenty-nine at the time. Thomas Brain lived with his wife and family at Euroclydon, some three miles from the colliery. He took pride in the fact that from a window of a tower attached to his house he could see the colliery; and if the smoke was rising from its chimneys he knew that the men were working.

In his diary Bill refers to William Blanch Brain as W.B.B., and Thomas Bennett Brain as T.B.B. William Brain was the most important man in the colliery in Bill's eyes, and he usually refers to him as *Mr* W.B.B.

There were other Brains working at Trafalgar: Walter John (referred to in the diary as Mr Walter), Charles Cornelius (referred to as C.C.B.) and Frank. These were cousins of various sorts. Walter, a bachelor, was the accountant who looked after the financial side of the business. C.C.B. was of more lowly rank and was only a few years older than Bill. Bill came into contact with him a lot and clearly did not get on with him. Frank Brain was a lad of sixteen when Bill began work at Trafalgar. Bill does not seem to have had much to do with him.

There is also mention in the diary of James or Jim Brain. He was a very distant relative of the owners of the colliery and was a pit manager, or bailiff as they were called. He was a keen chapel man. Even so, in the evenings he ran the Miners' Arms in nearby Hawsley.

William Brain seems to have been a colliery owner of the old-fashioned type found in Dean in the early years of the nineteenth century, one who actually worked in his colliery. He would arrive early in the morning, sometimes before 6.00 a.m., and was not averse to giving a hand in the store issuing tools to the men. From the diary entries he comes over as a friendly man, and Bill clearly got on well with him. We know from other sources, however, that he was a hard employer. The local Miners' Union agent, Timothy Mountjoy, once said that he was down at Trafalgar sorting out industrial disputes more than at any other pit in the Forest. Little industrial trouble is mentioned in the diary, but Bill's first words are 'Trafalgar works played'. Later one meets 'Trafalgar played today'. These are euphemisms for 'the colliery was closed' because the colliers were on strike.

More about Trafalgar Colliery and the Brain family can be found in the Appendix.

Bill's girlfriend was Rebecca Loveridge, and there are many references to her in the diary. He called her Beck. She was a servant at Wootton Hill Cottage, which was situated in a well-to-do area of Gloucester. Along with a fellow servant, Mary Nelmes, she lived in. The house was occupied by an old lady, Miss Witton, her two nieces, who were her 'companions', and her nephew, who was a solicitor. Beck and Mary looked after them, and a hard job they had of it, no doubt.

Our Bill had a roving eye and, in spite of his love for Beck, he reacted favourably to the blushes of the girls in the Forest of Dean. One cannot but smile at the revelations in the diary of his bouts of conscience after he had been flirting with Nellie or Bessie or Jane.

Bill lodged in Cinderford with William and Sarah Green, whose address was 'near the Baptist Chapel, Cinderford Woodside'. He paid them about £2 a month for board and lodging. Mrs Green seems to have had a waspish disposition and was inclined to pry into the affairs of her lodger; but she could also be a generous soul.

While he was working as a porter at Gloucester station, Bill lodged nearby at the house of Isaiah Morse, who also worked there as a railway team examiner. Bill became a great friend of Morse, who was a few years older than himself, and after his move to the Forest of Dean visited him almost every time he came to Gloucester. He was at his side when he was ill with smallpox, and Bill gives a touching account of Morse's death from the disease.

On his trips to Gloucester to visit Morse and Beck, Bill would sometimes seek out old colleagues at the railway station and have a pint with them. He usually travelled back on the mail train, which arrived at Newnham station after 1.00 a.m. Then there was a three mile slog through lonely fields and lanes back to Cinderford. Bill had to get up again at 5.30 a.m. and walk two miles through the Forest to Trafalgar. On occasion he arrived at work frozen or soaking wet.

Returning home after the late shift was much more enjoyable. He would often come down by the 'cart' with anything up to ten other workers. They would travel 'like lightning, down at Bilson in about four minutes'. The 'cart' was almost certainly a tram attached to a small steam engine that normally pulled coal trucks along the colliery's private tramway to Bilson near Cinderford. It was about a mile and a half from the colliery to Bilson, so the speed could not have been more than twenty-five miles an hour.

In the little spare time he had, Bill kept himself busy. One of his pastimes was carving and polishing walking sticks and gun stocks, a skill he may have acquired from George Herbert, who was a carpenter, and with whom he had lodged as a boy. He played the accordion, the piano, the violin, the banjo and the concertina (though how well we don't know), and he spent hours practising 'the tonic sol-fa', by which he meant learning the tunes of the songs for the choir he attended. He also tried his hand at composing, and he seems to have written some fiction called *The History of Lazy Dick*. On Sundays he went to chapel, though to which one depended on the girls he thought might be there, whom he could see home and who perhaps might invite him in for tea.

Bill also reached out for higher things. He read the local and national newspapers assiduously and took clippings of items he wanted to keep. His reading included Mason on *Self Knowledge* and Dr Todd's *Students' Guide*. He began to teach himself shorthand, or phonography as he called it. This was in the days before shorthand and typing were used in offices. After he had learned a little he began to write up small sections of the diary in it, usually criticisms of the sermons he heard on Sundays or his feelings about his girlfriends that he would not have wanted to be discovered by his landlady or any other unauthorized reader. It was an early form of Pitman's shorthand, difficult to transcribe, and it was necessary to consult an 1850 Pitman's primer to decipher it.

The range of the diary is restricted, comment being made only on the happenings at Trafalgar Pit and Cinderford, with the odd extension to Gloucester. One would have enjoyed Bill's views on, say, the activities in 1872 and 1873 of the prime minister, Gladstone; or on the troubles in Ireland, which, as ever, were engaging public attention at the time; or on the after-effects of the Franco-Prussian War; or even on the chaos caused at Gloucester station, a place dear to Bill's heart, when the Great Western Railway changed over in 1872 from wide gauge to standard gauge. Unfortunately he does not offer his opinions on such topics, though he no doubt, as an avid newspaper reader, held views on them.

Instead we get a glimpse of how the upper stratum of working-class people in Cinderford lived. We learn that they kept pigs, which they killed themselves; were religious; worked on 26 December; were musical; and ate bloaters for supper. The Green family, with whom Bill lived, were poor enough to need to take in a lodger, for the men were but manual workers at the ironworks. Yet they owned a piano and a violin, and one of the sons could afford to pay for piano lessons.

The diary also reveals that at Trafalgar relations between the various grades in the work hierarchy were friendly and not as

TRAFALGAR COLLIERY

rigid as one might expect. The pit managers and Bill would get together at dinner time and practise the tonic sol-fa. All in all the diary shows that, in this part of England at least, the Victorians of the 1870s were not so stuffy as we tend to think.

The entries in Bill's diary show that his handwriting was well formed and his vocabulary good. It is surprising to find that he used the old-fashioned *ſs* in, for example, *succeſs*. Once or twice he used an *ſ* for *s*, for example in *roſe* for *rose*. This means that the long s must have survived into the twentieth century. He wrote *ment* and *dropt* where we would write *mended* and *dropped*. He used *clean* where we would use *wash,* and *coin* where we would use *cash*. He frequently used adjectives where we would use adverbs, and he would say *they was* instead of *they were*. Some of these differences were regional dialect and some perhaps standard English of the time. His spelling was not good, though acceptable by modern standards; and if you take the trouble to check his sums you will find that his arithmetic was faulty at times. But whatever Mr Bradshaw failed to teach him at his school, he certainly taught him a good round hand and a facility to choose apt words.

Little remains today of Bill's world. Trafalgar House still stands, as does the upper office; they are now private residences. But what was left of the colliery was ruthlessly demolished, with little regard for the industrial archaeologist, by the Forestry Commission in 1986. Some of the shops Bill frequented in Cinderford remain, though none of the old names – Greenings, Woods, Longs and others – have survived over the shop fronts. The Cinderford Baptist Chapel is still there, much the same as it was in 1872. The Lower George at Newnham, where Bill took a drink while waiting for the Gloucester train, also survives, though it is no longer a public house.

The diary ends abruptly and with a twinge of underlying sadness, but we are left with the memory of a bright, observant, friendly young man with a zest for living. More important, perhaps, he reminds us that young men in the 1870s had the same thoughts and feelings as young men have in the 1990s.

Bill would be surprised to find his diary in print 120 years after he wrote it because, unlike many diarists, he did not intend it for publication. We hope that he would not be too upset (or vex'd, as he would have put it) because we have disclosed some of his innermost thoughts, for we also reveal him as a very likeable and interesting person.

Bess and Ralph Anstis
Coalway
Forest of Dean
Gloucestershire
September 1994

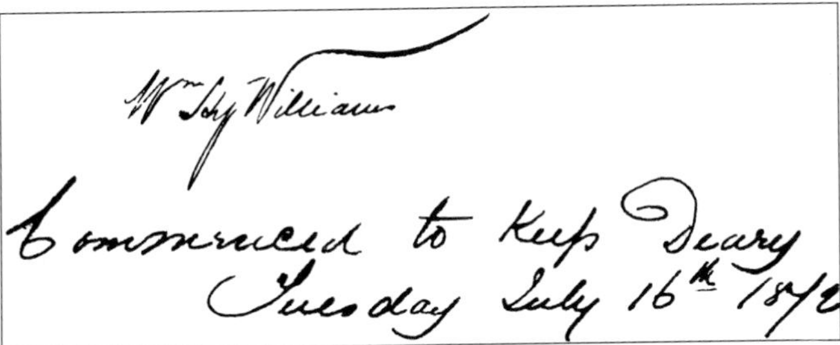

Tuesday July 16th

Trafalgar works play'd.[1] Bought two books, Dr. Todd's *Students' Guide* 1/– and Mason on *Self Knowledge* 1/–. Gardner Lewis[2] from Monmouth took tea with me at lodgings at Mrs. Green's, Cinderford.

2/–

Wednesday July 17th

Woke late in morning (6 a.m.) Works playing. Took state of tools out of book.

Bought book *Flashes of Light* and thimble case, ivory, off Gardner 8d. Lost knife.

Thursday July 18th

Woke at 5 a.m. Going in pit,[3] to compare tools with lists. <u>Countermanded</u>. Took tools out of old book. Odd work. Received letter from Beck.[4]

Friday July 19th

Woke at 5 a.m. Works playing. Halliday[5] spent about six hours with T.B. and W.B. Brain. Chapell[6] reprimanded stifly. Wrote Ashphelt Company for man or two to come when they come to Bristol. Wrote to coal merchants. After 6 p.m. painted dog's house red.

'Going in pit.'

Saturday July 20th

Pay. Men agitated. Many refused to sign for wages. Several meetings. Ed Cooksey[7] got into hot water for speaking against Warry.[8] Brought tickets from Mr. Walter for Weston-Super-Mare. Could not dispose of one at Cinderford. Bought suit of clothes £3/11/– of J. McKuskey.[9]

Paid £2 7*s* 0*d*

Sunday

July 1872

Spent day at home at lodging. Jim[10] stayed out all Saturday night. Came home after dinner on Sunday, exhausted. Sunday overwhelming hot. Went to Baptist Chapel at night. Very good minister. Text taken from *St. Luke* chapter XV verse 7th, 'For I say unto you that likewise joy shall be in Heaven over one sinner that repenteth.'

'Band gone to Weston-super-Mare.' *Trafalgar Colliery Band.*

Monday July 22nd 1872

Very hot. Band gone to Weston-Super-Mare in two break [brake] vans. Colliers all brought out their tools.[11] Self checked tools from the men. Mr. W.B.B. affected when band played off. They left about 7 a.m. Many of colliers affected. John Mason[12] and Harry Jenkins[13] went to Weston Super Mare. Self had tickets to sell. Sold two to Mr. South. Took parcell from Morgan.[14] Wrote Beck, remonstrative and affectionately. Forgot to post same day.

'Took telegram to post office.' *Cinderford's post office in the 1870s was housed in this building and was often used by Bill Williams. It had come down in the woeld by the 1950s when this photograph was taken.*

Tuesday July 23rd 1872

Parcell brought from Morgans for W.B.B. Wrote out statistic of toolls. Wrote Samuell Bros., London, for coachman's livery and hat. Also to National Provincial Bank for cheque book. Found two stamps for W.B.B. Hodges and W.B.B. holding debate at 6 p.m. Took telegram to post office, Cinderford, for Mr. Walter and note to McKuskey. Received letter from Morse.[15] Read in evening Todd's *Students' Manual*.

Wednesday July 24th 1872

Trafalgar silent. W.B.B. and Mr. Walter off for Illfracombe as I arrived. Few day men working. Smith, weighman at quarry, filling carts. Self worked at clearing up reciepts &c, docketing letters and assisting Johny Mason.

Came home, read, blew pipe of tobacco, played on accordion, mended trowsers. Bought *Graphic* from Cordwins.[16] Promised to meet Ruth Price[17] and fetcher home. Took second thought. Thought of Beck, stayed at home. Maria[18] in bad temper at bed time. Lads all at practice on brass instruments.

Spent *6d*

Thursday July 25th 1872

Took box and basket of fish from Morgan.[19] W.B.B. not up till 11 a.m. Went out in carriage about 12 p.m. Self assisted John Mason and talked. Not much work doing. Chappell nearly drunk. Mr. Walter did not come in office till dinner time.

Cleaned and did two walking sticks. Went to singing class. Mr. Waites[20] absent. Watched lightning till 10.30 p.m. Read none this evening.

Friday July 26th 1872

Mr. W.B.B. left home for two or three days before I got up to Trafalgar. Took out ledger accounts in upper office. Received letter from N. White, Newnham, who is going in business there. Thought of making arrangements for a share. Mason and I dined in my office. Gardner Lewis gave us four onions.

Came home about half past 5 p.m. Brought box for Morgan, to go to Gloster on Saturday.

Saturday July 27th 1872

Morn cool, day hot. Trafalgar still silent. Grand demonstration of colliers and unionists at Speech House.[21] Six bands reported to have been there. Self worked, taking out ledger account. Wrote two letters, one to Nicholson & Co., London, other to Horlick, Ross, enclosing cheque for both. Received 2d. for stamps.

Spent 1/1d. for tuning fork, 1d. for sweets. Read a little, washed and cleaned on Saturday night. To bed early before all the rest. Good resolution for Sabbath.

1/1*d*

'Grand demonstration of colliers and unionists at Speech House.' *This drawing of the Speech House in the centre of the Forest of Dean was made in 1858, but the building was much the same when the miners' first demonstration was held there in 1872.*

Sunday July 28th 1872

Read *Students' Manual of Exercise on Tonic Solfa* in morning. Cleaned after dinner. Went to Chapel at night. Mr. W.B.B. there taking notes. Spoke to me on leaving. Chapel crowded. Mr. Brown, Secretary of Amalgamated Association of Miners, preached. Tim Mountjoy[22] prayed. Text taken from *Luke XV* on the prodigal son. Text very good. Well adapted for young men about leaving home. Backsliders. Intended writing to White, but left till Monday.

Monday July 29th 1872

Stormy day. Warm. Men expecting to work. Disappointed. Meeting of men held near Briarley.[23] Warry given £20/–/– to take his hook. Put Cowmeadow to rule fresh book for tools.

Came home. Read *Science of Mining* through. Bought bottle of port 3/–, quinine 1/–. Paid McKusky £1/4/– for suit of clothes. Bill receipted. Came home. Practised on tonic sol-fa for an hour.[24] Ment trowsers. Arranged books for the morrow. Read chapter. Prayers and to bed.

Total spent £1/7/3

'Practised on tonic solfa for an hour.' *Traditional system of musical notation with tonic sol-fa alternative.*

Tuesday July 30th 1872

Morning wet. Very stormy all day.[25] Mr. W.B.B. quite in a fix over it. Sorting tools all day in stores. Left for home in evening about 5 p.m.[26] along with Mr. T.B.B., Harry Jenkins and John Mason. Took parcel from Morgans. Got wet through going to work and stayed in same clothes all day. Took medicine in morning and when I came home at 6.30 p.m.

Shaved, washed and learned shorthand an hour. Went to practice, tonic sol-fa for an hour and a half. Came home. Partook of bloater for supper. Read chapter. Prayers.

Wednesday July 31st 1872

Gave out rest of tools, Mr. W.B.B., Mason and Jenkins assisting. Men late going in pit. Cleaned up stores and re-arranged it till dinner time. Went in pit to book out first shift of men.[27] Offered

4/6d. per day by George Athey for filling.[28] About 50 men in second shift. Sent Mr. W.B.B. a note to save working all night.

Read phonography[29] all way coming home. Got loaf for C.C.B. Cautioned by H. Chip[30] for stepping off carriage till settled down on the fangs. Mrs. Green brewing. Fish arrived from Morgans for morning. Read Mason on *Self Knowledge* 1 hour, practised tonic sol-fa half hour, and read chapter from Philemon's *Prayers, Meditation and Self Examination*. Paid Maria 2d. for composite candle. Bed.

Spent 2*d*

Thursday August 1st 1872

Took fish to Trafalgar. Fine morning. Book'd men in pit. Late before all men was in. Went to ascertain some men's time for Mr. C.C.B. Failed. Sheets missing. Read Mason on *Self Knowledge* this morning. Book'd men out, came home early.

Received letter from Beckie. Jenkins and Mason came to Mrs. Green's to tea. Went towards the site of the children's fete. Supposed to be 600 at tea party. Rain came on at about 7 p.m. Did nothing at home. Read chapter from *Proverbs*. Said prayers. Meditation. Bed.

Friday August 2nd 1872

In pit booking men and comparing sheets. Wrote Beckie. Sent letter. Came home. Made modulator.[31] Did nothing beside. Bought 1d. postage stamp and three ½d. ones. Gave Mrs. Green half penny in fun to leave us.

P.S. Took loaf for C.C.B. in morning.

3d. spent

Saturday August 3rd 1872

Pay day. Received £2/4/-. Paid Mrs. Green for 4 weeks account £1/18/3. Bought *Budget, Police News*,[32] *Illustrated News*, also *The Identification of our Race* for John Miller.[33] Wrote him. Two pennyworth of pears, and lard 1d. Saw old Joe Cook. Talked few minutes. Received box from Morgan for Trafalgar. Went to

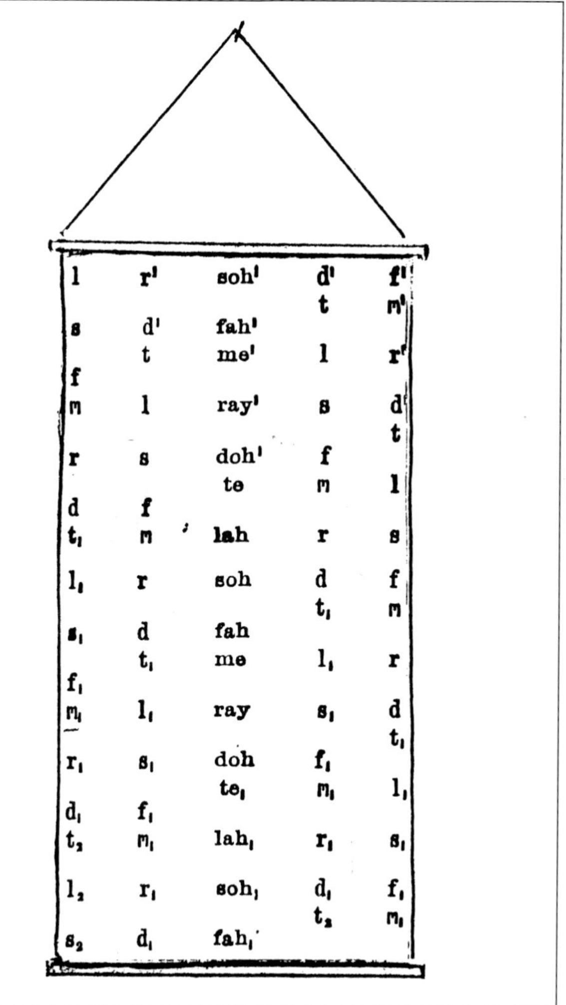

'Made modulator.'

Kitsills to enquire about sheets. Spent some time with Gardner, the gas man, talking matters over and suggesting arrangements for future experiments [with gas].

Home very late. Took supper, had cucumber. Prayers and to bed. Slept with Bill. No reading done.

£	s.	d.
2	4	0
1	19	1
	14	1

'Very poor sermon. Same as usual from poor Preece.' *Phillip Prees, pastor of Cinderford Baptist Chapel.*

Sunday August 4th 1872

Spent Sunday very ill. Late rising. Read papers most of day. Day bright and clear in morning, dull in afternoon. John and William using very pungacious strains in morning over a drop of water spilt in back kitchen. Read tonic a little in afternoon. Kitsill came in morning and I borrowed binocular glass. Saw Trafalgar plainer than ever before from bedroom window. Saw rope on deep pit quite distinctly.

Went to Chapel in evening. Preece preached from *Epistle of St. John*. Very poor sermon. Same as usual from poor Preece.[34] Was thinking in Chapel of learning shorthand and go and take the Revd. Bennett's sermon of Hereford. Very many times thought wandering to sin and world. Broke resolution. Read, took no supper, prayers and to bed.

Monday Aug. 5th 1872

Wet morn. C.C.B. booked men in pit. Worked all day after in pit at examining sheets, revizing books &c. Came home at 6 p.m. Wrote shorthand few minutes. Went out through wood to meet Maria coming from [Little] Dean. Black day, missed her, she home first. Talked a bit. Took physic and to bed.

Tuesday Aug. 6th 1872

Fine morn. Smith not arrive till 7 a.m. Harry Jenkins had to weigh. Work'd down in pit all day. Came home with Emily Green, housemaid, who had just left Trafalgar. She took tea with me. Went to Mr. Burrows and on the hill her father was there waiting for her. Quite a youthfull, fine looking fellow. Bought cake for her, 10d.

Went to [music] class, learning transition. Mrs. Green made 2 pint bottles of medicine. Gave me the reciept. Wrote out same from hers.

Spent 10d.

Wednesday Aug. 7th 1872

Dull and wet, cold and miserable. Self booked colliers into pit.

C.C.B. in pritty good [humour] all day. Have not seen Mr. W.B.B. all the week. Break [brake] of dipple[35] engine broken last night.

Rode home on engine[36] with C.C.B. Fetched tobacco paper and pamphlet on the *Failure and Career of Napoleon* from Cordwins. Paid Mr. Long 1d., binding book 10d. Looked at makintosh at McKuskeys. He offered it for 12/–. Received very kind letter from Beck. Bought two stamps for paper and one ½d. one. Bought rolls for C.C.B. Spoke to Gardner on opening fish business here. Sent John Miller *The Identification of the Lost House of Israel*. Called by old Joe Cooks.

Been very wicked this evening. Cursed and swore several times. Discussed solemn matters very slightly. Read a little. No supper. Smoked part of a cigar presented me by Samuel[37] from Bristol. To bed.

Thursday August 8th 1872

Took fish from Morgans. Took rolls for C.C.B. Book'd colliers into pit. Weigh'd till 7 a.m. Squared sheets. Could not get electric machine to act. Fresh orders to take to stores again. Absence of leave granted for one day, Monday, provided arrangements can be made. Mr. Walter spinning yarn at weighbox about 6 p.m.

Came home part of way with W. Harris. Met Trotter's shop girls. Went back and over pit with them. Received insult from W. Harris. Took it quite calmly. Frank Brain's watch at Greenings[38] to be called for, but being Thursday shops at Cinderford all shut.

Came home towards 9 p.m. No-one at home. All gone to see efigy being burnt. Got out wig for party. No reading or writing. Went to bed late. Thought of writing to Gloster to Morse and Beck. Postponed till morrow. Bed &c &c &c.

Friday August 9th 1872

Book'd colliers. Work'd in pit. Learned some of store books. Wrote note about Pogson[39] allowing men to ascend without ticket.[40] Wrote Beck and Morse.

The identity disc of a Trafalgar collier.

Bedsteads.

Iron and Brass Bedsteads, Children's Cots, Folding Chairs, and Bedsteads, also Palliasses & Mattresses for the same.

Ranges, Stoves, &c.

Kitchen Ranges, with open or close Fire, with wrought-iron Boilers, for supplying Hot Water upstairs to Bath, &c.

Register Stoves, Fenders, and Fire-Irons.

Lamps.

Moderator, Solar, Reading, and Hall Lamps, Chimnies, Globes, and Wicks.

Best French Colza Oil.

Best Crystal Oil for Petroleum Lamps.

Baths.

Hip, Sponging, Traveling, & Shallow Baths, Toilet Sets, Hot Water Cans, &c.

Garden Requisites.

Lawn Mowers, Rollers, Syringes, Watering Pots, Garden Engines, Water Barrows. Hand Glass Frames, Garden Chairs and Seats, in Wood and Iron.

Brushes.

Carpet Sweepers, Bass and House Brooms; Scrubbing, Stove, Shoe, Plate, Cloth, Crumb, Flue, and Hat Brushes.

WILLIAM WOOD,

IRONMONGER,

CINDERFORD.

Electro-Plated Goods.

Forks, Spoons, Tea and Coffee Services, Cruet Frames, Liquor Frames, Biscuit Boxes, Butter Dishes, Dessert Knives and Forks, Nut Crackers, Grape Scissors, &c.

Cutlery.

Table Knives & Forks with Ivory, Stag, or Bone Handles; Scissors, Pen and Pocket Knives, Razors, Bread Knives, Cooks' Knives and Steels.

Culinary Articles.

Saucepans, Stew Pans, Kettles, Fry Pans, Gridirons, Fish Kettles, Boilers, Moulds, Warren's Cooking Pots & Mincing Machines.

Workmen.

Experienced Workmen employed in the following branches:— Plumbing, Gas-Fitting, Bell-Hanging, Smithing, and Tin-Plate Working.

Miscellaneous.

Copper Prickers, for Blasting Purposes; Miners' Lamps in Brass and Tin, Cast-Iron Spouting, &c., &c.

Tin & Japan Goods.

Tea Trays, Waiters, Coal Scoops and Vases, Foot and Carriage Warmers; Cash, Jewel, and Deed Boxes; Nursery Lamps, &c.

'Brought note to Woods.' Morris & Co.'s Commercial Directory of Gloucestershire, 1876.

Brought note to Cordwins and Woods.[41] Bought two stamps. Bought makintosh from McKuskey's 12/–. Not paid for. Bought small box for sundries in bedroom from Longs.[42] Brought order from Cordwins. Mrs. Green at club. Had meat and glass of milk for supper. Read, arranged about trip to Gloster, shaved, &c. Bed.

Spent 12/4d.

Saturday August 10th 1872

Got time-off sheets for the week. Left Trafalgar about 4 p.m. Cleaned, got ready and went to Gloster and got to Newnham at 6 p.m. Walked down with Preece, the auctioneer. Quite enjoyed his company. Drank glass of whiskey and gingerade with him at Lower George, Newnham. Rode up to Gloster with Tocknell.

Arrived in Gloster about 8 p.m. Went across to wagon office. Saw Joe, William, Frank, John, on duty, Mark Wheeler, Dick Porter. Went up to Wootton Hill Cottage.[43] Quite delighted to see Beck and she me. Slept there on Saturday night. Got to bed about 1 a.m. Bought [a false shirt] front 1/2d., cuffs 1/2d., gloves 2/9d., box of collars 6d. Never took Beck anything. Borrowed umbrella of Wootton Hill Cottage.

Spent 6/6d.

Sunday Aug. 11th 1872

Shied up about 8 a.m. Mary[44] went to Cheltenham in morning per first train. Beck and I stayed at Wootton Hill Cottage. Went

'Got to Newnham at 6 p.m.' *A view of the Severn above Newnham. Bill Williams would have had this view when walking from Cinderford to Newnham station.*

'Morse and I lunched in Westgate Street.'

Short Trains Glou. to Chelt. : 8 15 .. 12 38p.m. & 2 35 5 0 .. 6 35 .. 10 30 .. 11 20 p.m. & 12 40.

SOUTH WALES RAILWAY.
CHELTENHAM AND GLOUCESTER TO MILFORD HAVEN.

SUNDAYS.

Departur from	3dCl. a. m.	3dCl. a. m.	3dCl. a. m.	3dCl. a. m.	3dCl. p. m.	3dCl. p. m.	Exp. p. m.	Mail. a. m.	Mail. p. m.	3dCl. a. m.	3dCl. p. m.
Cheltenham........	5 35	6 55	10 15	1 15	2 0	5 45	7 55	12 5	12 5	7 45	1 15
Gloucester..........	6 0	7 45	10 45	1 42	3 0	7 15	8 20	12 50	12 50	8 10	3 30
Oakle Street........	..	7 57	10 57	..	3 15	7 23	..	..	..	8 21	3 42
Grange Court	6 15	8 3	11 3	..	3 20	7 30	..	..	..	3 30	3 47
Newnham..........	6 23	8 13	11 13	2 2	3 30	7 40	..	1 12	1 12	8 40	3 57
Awre (for Blakeney)..............	..	8 20	11 22	..	3 40	7 49	..	..	..	8 48	4 5
Lydney............	6 40	8 32	11 36	2 19	3 55	8 8	..	1 31	1 31	9 2	4 19
Woolaston..........	..	8 40	11 44	..	4 5	8 11	..	..	..	9 10	4 27
Chepstow..........	6 55	8 54	11 58	2 34	4 20	8 25	9 5	1 49	1 49	9 23	4 40
Newport............	7 35	9 48	12 45	3 7	5 5	9 15	9 40	2 21	2 21	10 10	5 25
Cardiff	8 5	10 20	1 20	2 35	5 40	9 40	10 5	2 45	2 45	10 45	6 0
Llantrissant........	8 27	10 52	1 55	..	6 15	——	..	..	..	11 13	6 33
Bridgend............	8 52	11 15	2 18	4 10	6 45	stop	10 40	3 20	8 20	11 37	7 0
Port Talbot........	9 20	11 44	2 48	4 33	7 18		..	3 44	3 44	12 6	7 28
Neath..............	9 42	12 5	3 9	4 46	7 45		11 15	3 57	3 57	12 22	7 46
Swansea	9 50	12 15	3 15	4 50	7 55		11 20	5 45	5 45	——	7 55
Llanelly	10 33	12 58	4 7	5 28	8 46		11 58	4 5	4 5		8 47
Carmarthen Junc..	11 30	1 47	5 5	6 15	9 40		12 38	5 25	5 25		9 37
Whitland, for Tenby	12 5	——	——	6 47	——		..	5 50	5 50		10 13
Narberth Road for Cardigan	12 18	stop	stop	..	stop		..	..	..		10 24
Haverfordwest	12 43			7 20			1 35	6 26	6 20		11 5
Milford Haven *arr.*	1 15			7 45			1 55	6 50	6 50		11 20

A timetable of the South Wales Railway, by which Bill Williams travelled between Newnham and Gloucester. Note that 'the mails' left Gloucester at 12.50 a.m.

out in morning to see Morse. Not in. Saw Rowland {Morse} and then returned to Wootton Hill Cottage to dinner at 1.10 p.m. Came on to rain. Went to telegraph to Mary to return after dinner. Telegraph not working that day.

Beck and I went to Cheltenham in afternoon. Saw Gardner Lewis at station. Spoke but a little. Fare for Beck and I 2/–. Met Mary close to Keynsham St. Returned all together. Miss Witton[45] worse and returns on Monday. Took tea together at Wootton Hill Cottage. Mary went out and Beck and I stayed at home. I wrote to Mrs. Roberts for Beck. Slept at Wootton Hill Cottage. Got to bed about 12 midnight.

Spent 2/–

Monday Aug. 12th 1872

Rolled out at 8.30 a.m. Beck and I and Mary breakfasted all together. Left Wootton Hill Cottage about 10 a.m. Boy[46] didn't know I slept there. Went to Morses. Spent an hour or two. Morse and I went round town. Bought toys for children 1/6d., fruit 6d., cup for Mrs. Morse 7d. Morse and I lunched in Westgate St. 2/–. Bought four pictures in Eastgate St. (Spring, Summer, Autumn, Winter), 2/–, and six comic C.D.V.s[47] for Beck 3/–. Collected all pictures together and gave them Beck.

In evening conversed about going to pit work. Beck does not approve of it at all. Called at Peter's[48] house. He came with Beck and I to Wootton Hill Cottage. Mary went out. Peter's wife unwell. Beck suffering occasionally from toe. Stayed till mails.[49]

Came to station before midnight. Spent 6d. at Vaughxhall with Morse. Called at Gloster Hotel. Spent 1/1½d. there with Morse and Reuben and Tom Stevens. Talked to Morse on platform. Got ticket, 11d., to Newnham. Walked home after 1.20 a.m. Got home at 2.15 a.m. Frightened most infernally by a herd of neddies. Went straight to bed at 2.35.

Spent 12/1 at Gloster

Tuesday Aug. 13th 1872

Smith book'd men in pit. Went up about 8 a.m. C.C.B. not

there. Mac and I arranged sheets, etc. Mr. W.B.B. engaged in confab with Pogson, R. Jay and John Hale about the note C.C.B. preferred me to tell him [W.B.B.] of instead of himself. C.C.B. not here today. Took penny loaf for him.

Came home about 5 p.m. Practised at class. Oafed[50] a little with a visitor of Mrs. Green's (Sally Baggs). Bill took her home or somewhere. Went to bed, came down and read *Alonzo the Brave* to those left up. Went off to bed just before 12 p.m. midnight. No prayers.

Bought paper, *Beehive*[51] 2d.

Wednesday August 14th 1872

Book'd colliers in pit. Self had narrow escape of a cut on the

'Frightened most infernally by a herd of neddies.'

hand. Slight grazed by axe falling down out of weighbox. Mr. Roberts nearly caught by same. C.C.B. arrived when we were at dinner. No gas all day scarcely or yesterday either. Kitsill left paper for Mr. Walter, said he had berth at Cardiff at 32/– per week as a storekeeper. Showed me Mr. Brain's testimonial. Wanted to borrow coin. William Henry Williams not to be had. Mr Halliday expected at Trafalgar all day, though not arrived at 5 p.m.

Left pit about 5 p.m. Smith, Ennis and John Hale holding love feast.[51] Rode home on Collon's engine. Took tin to Bouds[53] to have handle put on. Called at Woods for screws for handle of doors, 20 of them, for Mr. W.B.B. Saw Mr. and Mrs. W.B.B. drive by in carriage whilst there, Conolly[54] behind. Mr. W.B.B. went in to Cordwins, Mrs. W.B.B. kept seat. Saw Ted Wilks from Gloster. Shook hands with him. Bought snuff and candle.

D. Clarke came here and practised on modulator. Read chapter from Collossian's *Prayers* and turned in. Wished Beck there along.

3d.

'Rode home on Collon's Engine.' *This tank engine, normally pulled twenty to twenty-five trams of coal at a time to Bilson, near Cinderford, where the coal was transferred to the trucks of the Great Western Railway. Maybe Charles Collon, its driver, is standing on the footplate.* See note 36.

Thursday Aug. 15th 1872

Shied up at 5.30 a.m., hurried to Trafalgar. Took fish from Morgans, screws from Woods. Book'd men in pit, all in early. Took time-off sheets. Did not compare books with C.C.B. Clear'd up sheets. Did not bring C.C.B.'s bread – shops shut. Wrote Morse and Beck.

Bought stamps 8d. Gave Lizie[55] 1d. Practised on tonic. Maria's birthday, 17 years. Bess Morgan left parcel forgotten yesterday. Red chapter from *Ephesians*. Prayers. Roll'd in at 10.30. Amen.

Friday Aug. 16th 1872

Morn dull and wet. Book'd men in pit. Weighed till 8 a.m. Got books square. Wrote Beck and Morse. Took parcel for Morgans. Forgot C.C.B.'s bread, cadged some from house for him. Kitsill tried to borrow 1/2d. for W. Harris. Couldn't see that. Sorry, but no go.

Came home. Bought tobacco pouch and paper 1/3½d., *Foresters* 3d., *Identity of Lost House* 4d., stamps 3d. Had confab with Mr. Long about fish business at Cinderford. Mr Long strongly recommends a dash at it. Asked me to buy some books, Josephus &c, a bargain. Promised to bear it in mind. Mrs. Long sadly perplexed about her lost cat. Bought snuff from Cordwins. 1d. paid for bread for C.C.B.

'Bought *Foresters* 3d.'

The Forester,

COLEFORD, CINDERFORD, AND EAST & WEST DEAN ADVERTISER,
LYDNEY, NEWNHAM, BLAKENEY, AND MONMOUTH GAZETTE.

VOL. XIII—No. 640 [Registered for Transmission Abroad.] FRIDAY, SEPTEMBER 13, 1872. [Registered at the General Post-Office as a Newspaper.] Price THREE-HALFPENCE.

JOHN COLEMAN,
Auctioneer, Valuer,
HOUSE, ESTATE, MINERAL, & INSURANCE AGENT,
Licensed Victuallers' Broker; Rent, Tithe, and Debt Collector, and General Accountant,
HIGH STREET, COLEFORD, Gloucestershire.

AGENT to the LIVERPOOL, LONDON, and GLOBE FIRE and LIFE INSURANCE COMPANY; and the RAILWAY PASSENGERS ASSURANCE COMPANY against Accidents of all kinds.

Valuations for Probate, Legacy, and Succession Duties.

DESIRABLE FREEHOLDS IN THE FOREST OF DEAN

CHARLES WILSON

CHARLES ROBERTS,
Auctioneer, Appraiser, Valuer, and House Agent.
COLEFORD.

Immediate Settlement of all Accounts,

Offices: Newland Street, Coleford.

TO BE LET (Unfurnished), TUMP HOUSE, Coleford.—Apply to Mr. Chas. Roberts, Auctioneer, Coleford.

Alliance Life & Fire Assurance Company.
CAPITAL, £5,000,000.

AGENT, Mr. RICHARD JACKSON, Solicitor, Cinderford.—Office hours 9 till 7 daily.

FURNITURE, CARPETS, BEDDING
LAVERTON & CO.'S
STEAM CABINET WORKS,
MARY-LE-PORT STREET, BRISTOL.

LAVERTON & CO.'S IMMENSE STOCK of MODERN FURNITURE comprises the Largest Variety in the West of England, manufactured at their own Steam Cabinet Factory, warranted all of Good Quality and Workmanship, at Prices Moderate.

LAVERTON & CO.'S IMMENSE STOCK of CARPETS and DAMASKS

Enlargement of Premises at Newerne, Lydney.

CONTINUANCE OF THE
Great Sale of Drapery and Outfittings, for another Week.
FURTHER REDUCTION ON ALL SUMMER GOODS.

JAMES DICKS, Proprietor.

SPEECH HOUSE HOTEL,
Near COLEFORD.

JOHN SMITH

"ALLAN" ROYAL MAIL LINE.
SHORTEST SEA PASSAGE

TO CANADA and the UNITED STATES.—Shortest Route to the West.

From LIVERPOOL to QUEBEC.

Lizie got a hiding at bedtime. Went to bed early. Read out of *Proverbs*. Thought of writing to T.W.O.,[56] Monmouth.

Spent 2/6½d.

Saturday Aug 17th 1872

Beautiful day for the pay. Book'd men in pit before 6 a.m. Squared up pit books. C.C.B. not in pit all day, he was wanted with pay. Received £2/3/3. Paid Mason £1/–/– borrowed. Received orders to take charge of stores on Monday. Mr. W.B.B.'s office going all behind with work. Hodges, Morgan and W.B.B. and T.B.B. holding confab in upper office. Halliday down on Friday to settle colliers' dispute. Left Trafalgar at 4.15 p.m.

Received letter from Mrs. Morse. Charlotte Cooksey called. Sparked with Bess Morgan. Bought hair oil 4d., sweets 1½d., pipe tubes 2d. Home at 12 p.m. midnight. No prayers again. Good night, Amen.

Spent £1/0/7

Sunday Aug. 18th 1872

Sunday beautiful day, very hot in afternoon. Went to Chapel in morning. Beautiful sermon. Stringer preached text from *Proverbs* 'Keep thine own heart, for out of it are the issues of life.'

'Was invited to accompany them to Flaxley Abbey in afternoon.'

Introduced to Miss Cook.[57] Was invited to accompany them to Flaxley Abbey in afternoon. Started at 2 p.m. Clarke, Mr. & Mrs. Cook, two sisters and self. Arrived too late for Church. Went in after service was over. Beautiful interior, resembled Highnam.[58] All of it like T.G. Parry's work.

Called at a Mrs. Drew on wayside home. Took bread and butter, fowl and tea. Passed by group of boys bathing in St. Anthony's Well.[59] Self gathered nosegay for Miss Cook, nuts &c, not ripe though. Tea cost 1/–. Wonder'd about Beck. Wished Beck had been there to make party complete.

Interview and short conversation with Miss Cook's uncle from Nailsworth or Shortwood. He knows George Bishop well. Very pious.

Went took second tea with David Clark. Beautiful tea, very pleasant conversation. Went for a walk after tea by Steam Mill and back through wood. Saw Mr. W.B.B. and family driving home from Chapel, Mr. Walter and W.B.B. blowing cigars. Time about 9.30 p.m.

Hasted home. Invited at any time to Miss Cook's at Cheltenham.[60] Took adieu. Home at 11.40. All a-snoring at lodge. Prayers in bed. Amen.

Spent 1/–

Monday Aug. 19th 1872

Beautiful day, hot. Arrived at 6.40 and no Pogson to start. Took to stores. Mr W.B.B. up and wrote on the stores door 'No Storekeeper'. C.C.B., looking in on top of pit in morning, had books and diary for ropes brought out of pit. Felt quite sleepy early part of day in stores. Charlotte Cooksey to come to Trafalgar [House] tomorrow. Chapel gone off for a trip to Wootton-under-Edge. Ruth [Price] wanted me to accompany her to Shakemantle.[61] Not for me.

Came home at 5 p.m. Commenced to make a bonfire. Intended to write but postponed it for a few days till fresh thoughts burst forth. Mrs. Green and Maria busy washing. No reading or writing in own time. Prayed in bed.

'Arrived too late for church.' *Flaxley church.*

'Passed by group of boys bathing in St. Anthony's Well.'

Tuesday

Stores today very hot. Mr. Walter unwell. Brought phial bottles from Cordwins for him. Bought bottle of lemonade and camels hair brush 3½d., 2 paint tins 1/–. Done bit to banjoe. Went to practice. Got on very bad. No reading or anything. John and Jim nearly tight. John off to Chipstow Flower Show tomorrow. Prayers in bed.

2/3½d.

KAYE'S WORSDELL'S PILLS.

This invaluable Medicine has been in use for the last half century with the most unqualified success. They act upon the liver without mercury, and cleanse the stomach and bowels without weakening them, remove the causes that in different constitutions occasion giddiness and pains in the head, sickness at the stomach, fever, indigestion, influenza, rheumatism, or gout, and so ward off those attacks of disease that lead to so much suffering and expense.

Sold by all Chemists and other Dealers in Patent Medicines, at 1*s.* 1½*d.*, 2*s.* 9*d.*, *and* 4*s.* 6*d.*

Wholesale Depot: 22 Bread Street, LONDON.

'Mr Walter unwell. Brought phial bottles from Cordwins for him.' Slater's Directory, 1868.

Wednesday Aug. 21st 1872

Book'd few men in pit. Then Smith come and I took to stores. Mr. T.B.B. there early. Charlotte Cooksey come to live in the house. Took two paint kettles and two brushes there, paint bottles &c. Mr.W.B.B. taken ill in upper office. Mr. Griffiths there from Mitcheldean. Promised to bring book.

Paid for indiarubber coat 12/–. Measured for another pair of trowsers. Fetched fish from Morgan's. John Green and T.W. Harris gone to Chipstow Flower Show. William and I practised one hour and a quarter on tonic sol-fa. Bought bottle of port wine 2/3d. Gave Mrs. Green small tumbler full. She was very talkative before bedtime. Read a little. Prayers and bed.

14/3d.

P.S. Took sketch of elbows of pipe for ventilating pit to Boud to be done by Friday evening.

Thursday

Book'd men down. In stores all day. Did not see Mr. W.B.B. all day. Went in house in morning, chaffed girls.

Took fish from Morgans, bought varnish from Edwards 2/–, bought 1d. camel hair brush. Tonic a little, cleaned and pollish'd eight walking sticks. Bed. Bad day.

2/1d.

Friday Aug. 23rd 1872

Took varnish for Trafalgar engine. Book'd in men in pit.

Ordered some things from Mr. Boud. Bought paper from Mr. Cordwin 4d. Took 3d. book as specimen for inspection on appro. Took glass of ale along with Mr. Boud at publick house opposite. Promised to arrange orders for him all as lie in my power. Saw Miss Cook going down by when talking to Mr. Boud about 9.15 p.m. Returned home. Finished bottle of wine this day. Gave John strong cup of tea. Partook of cucumber, and off to bed. Prayers in bed.

Saturday Aug. 24 1872

Very hot, beautiful. Took books from Cordwins. Saw Mr. W.B.B. looking very ill. Had a lark with servants. In stores all day, posting.

Left at 2.30 p.m. Thoughts ran very freely. Practised on accordion good while. Not read at all. Thoughts continually prompting me to write to T.W.O. Stained banjoe. Paid for paper

'Thoughts continually prompting me to write to T.W.O.' *Lydart House, near Monmouth, family home of Thomas William Oakley, Bill Williams's father.*

1½d., logwood 1d. Gave Oliver[62] 3d. Partook of cucumber, ment trowsers &c. To bed.

Sunday Aug. 25th 1872

Rose about 9 a.m. Breakfast. Read Mason on *Self Knowledge.* Thought. Played on accordion. Did not clean or go out in morning. Dined off lamb, mint sauce, kidney beans and plum pie. Drank beer. Read no scripture today. Went to bed in afternoon. Lay till half past five p.m. Changed, went to Wesleyan Chapel. Text from *St. Mathew*, 'Seek ye first'.

Wed. Aug 28th 1872

Lovely day. Stores till evening. Went in pit with Ruth and Charlotte little past 4 p.m. Came out at a quarter to six p.m.

Weigh'd in night turn. Chapel and I had our tea down at house. Mr. W.W.B. out from home. Girls all got up after they were a-bed, and Mr. Walter in shirt sleeves talked to gals through window. Watched silent moves all night. Paid for three quarts beer 6d. to draw off Jenkins. All girls having fling proper. Ennis, Chappel and Jarrat together hold black love feast.

Book'd men out. Rode home in cart alone. Home at 2.30 a.m.

Total spent 10d.

Thursday

Mr. W.B.B. and Mrs. from home. Work'd in weighbox an hour at change of shift. Talked to Griffiths, Mitcheldean, borrowed book of him. He told anecdote of dream of his son concerning the death of men killed in the Plump [Hill quarry] explosion.[63] He came part of way home. Met Boud and turned back to put his tins in stores. Smoked a pipe. Bed at half past nine.

Friday Aug. 30th 1872

Rose late. Quarter past six when I got to Trafalgar. Henry Smith passed some remark about stores not being opened. Smith in weighbox want'd me to book men in on Saturday. Thought to have wrote Beck, but too busy. Borrow'd book off Mr. John Griffiths, Mitcheldean. Busy making posting book all day.

Went to try range of voice at Chapel. Tenor is my part. William Green is bass. Read McKuskey case about his bigamy. Bought bottle of Japan [lacquer] for C.C.B. Used drop for tea tray for Mrs. Green. Bought *Forester*, pipe stem for C.C.B., sweets 2½d. Bed half past ten p.m.

Total 5d.

Saturday Aug. 31st

Last day. Wet at intervals. Pay. Received £2/3/– as wages. Mr. W.B.B. not there. T.B.B. in upper office when I left. Borrowed book of Mr. Jno Griffiths, Mitcheldean, about infidels. Did not promise to return it at any set time. Spoke to Ruth Price when leaving about getting up in the night.[64]

Came home about five. Practised tonic sol-fa half an hour. Went out, met with John Morris, blacksmith. Spent 1/1d. for two quarts beer, 1d. pears. McKuskey sent home trowsers. Did not call to pay. McKuskey had name in paper over two wives this week. Read a little. Sent paper to Beck and letter containing 10/6d. for my book, *History of Franco-Prussian War*. Did not register letter or send order.

Total 11/10d.

Sunday September 1st 1872

Rose late, say nine or little past. Read some of Griffiths book. Learned tonic. Dined of lamb, kidney beans and plum pie. Paid Mrs. Green £1/14/10 for month's board. Went to Chapel in evening. Text taken from *St. Luke*. Poor sermon by P. Preece. Collection, gave 3d. Home, read out of *Proverbs* and *Revelation*. Took supper. Bed early, 10.15 p.m. John at home this week.

Total 11/1d.

Monday September 2nd

Wore new fustian trowsers. Forgot loaf for C.C.B., took portion of bread for him. Spoke to Mr. W.B.B. Delivered up diaries and memo. Thought of future prospects. Arranged with Smith about working two turns a week in his place, Wednesday and Fridays. Spoke to Ruth in morning. Washed poor old Boxer's wound, oil'd and bandaged it up. Begg'd rags from girls at house. Thought about Beck many times. Read very interesting *Almanac* of Professor O.P. Brown, No. 2 King Street, Covent Garden, London. Thought of attacking phonography again. Bought tobacco 9d., glue 6d. Commenced afresh at banjoe. Did not work long. Bed very late 11.10 p.m. No prayers.

Total spent 1/3d.

Tuesday

In stores making posting book. Mr W.B.B. up early. Jenkins came at quarter to 8 a.m. W.B.B. wanted to know if he was ill. Sent away forty sacks to J. & T. Robinson and box of fossils[65] for London firm. Mr. Walter sent ten tins for repair to Bouds. Told by W.B.B. should be required to write a letter for him. Did not hear any more about it.

Mr W.B.B. had company, Marlings[66] family from by Stroud.

Trimmed lamp for W.B.B. The Marlings visited pit with W.B.B. and some men. Spoke to Jane in morning. Spoke to Mrs. W.B.B. in evening and made slight boor.[67]

Came home, practised on piano. Show'd my accordion to some young man. Maria put riband round my hat. Self offered to do Maria's marking.[68] Mrs. Green baked. Practised at class. Mr. Waites tells us we improve fast. No letter. 4d. loaf for C.C.B. Partook of pie for supper. John and James up. Bed at 11 p.m.

4d.

Wednesday Sept. 4th 1872

Very stormy and wet much of the day and night. Late 15 minutes in the stores. Mr. W.B.B. wrote on my door, 'Storekeeper ill,' but was in excellent spirits, up at 6 a.m. and cutting about like a wild Irishman. W.B.B. worked in pit. Self forgot to send in day's tally.[69] Work'd for Smith after 5 p.m., made agreement with him to work his turn for 3/4d. a turn and do two turns per week and he the rest. Mr. W.B.B. told me to call for parcell for Morgan to take to Gloster. Mrs. Brain wanted to know where I was going and what for. Ruth Price's birthday, 21. Had glass of port and slice of cake to commemorate the same, wishing her all felicity, and many anniversaries of the same.

Rode home in cart. Fled down and four more beside. No supper or reading. Bed as soon as possible. Mrs. Green brewed and baked.

Thursday Sept. 5th 1872

Woke late, rose late. Took up fish from Morgan. Mr. W.B.B. busy, cutting about early. Door written on, 'No Storekeeper'. Felt rather annoyed. Very hard and busy day with iron &c. Mosooo[70] and W.B.B. at work in his office like one o'clock. Left at 5 p.m. Left tally today.

Came home, made hoop for Mrs. Green's wash tub. Took tickets for Independent Chapel tea meeting to Marfell, haulier &c, Cinderford, from Jim Brain. Partook of beer out of a double handed pispot. Came home, received letter and photo from my

GLOUCESTER AND STROUD ADVERTISEMENTS. 37

ABRAHAM THOMAS,

PHOTOGRAPHIC ART STUDIO,

3, St. John's Villas, Worcester St., Gloucester,

FIRST-CLASS CARTES DE VISITE

Vignettes, Miniatures for Pins, Rings, Brooches, and Lockets.

ENLARGEMENTS TO LIFE SIZE,

IN SEPIA, OIL, AND WATER COLORS.

VIEWS OF ALL SIZES. PORTRAITS TAKEN IN ALL WEATHERS.

'Kissed dear Beck's C.D.V. many times.' Morris & Co.'s Commercial Directory of Gloucestershire, 1865–66.

poor dear old gal, thoughts running on days passed for ever away. Kissed dear Beck's C.D.V. many times, many many times, hoping she will be able to remain for winter there [Gloucester]. Next spring we must be one, if possible. Prayed, read chapter from *Jude*. Meditated, and bed before John Green came home.

Friday Sept 6th 1872

Rose early. At Trafalgar before 6 a.m. Hung a piece of chalk outside door for W.B.B. to chalk the door with, but he took no notice of it. W.B.B. looked wicked at me and laughed when he saw me. Very busy in stores all day. Was in office in the house, received instructions about oil olive. Brought lamp to Woods to send to Birmingham for repairs. Called at Greenings for jewellry for Mrs. Brain. Wrote Dr. Evans, Reading, for advice medical for Mr. W.B.B. Spoke to postman about leaving my letter, then addressed letter to O. Williams[71] and posted it. Spent 2/6d. in ½d. stamps – Rhodes[72] had no penny ones. Bought paper from Longs 1½d., sweets 1½d., pop 1d., pictures 1/–, book cover 5/–. Home, read *Forester* a bit, looked over Morgan's bill £2/11/11 for Mr. Brain to take up in morning. Bed at 10.30 p.m. No prayers, no chapter.

6/4d. spent.

Saturday Sept. 7th 1872

Rose late, got to Trafalgar at 6.20 a.m., door chalked with men's names waiting for me. Painted door before breakfast. Stores all day till 3 p.m. Posted up some of old work. Talked to Griffiths, Mitcheldean, some while. Mr. Walter coming on Monday to inspect stores. His head is very bad today. Borrowed book of John Mason (Todd's *Self Improvement*).

Came home, bought papers, *Reynolds* and *Budget*. Hoop'd Mrs. Green's wash tub, ment chain. Read, played, exercised a little on tonic sol-fa. Went to bed. No prayers again.

'Spent 2/6d in ½d stamps – Rhodes had no penny ones.' *William Frowan Rhodes was Cinderford's first postmaster.*

Sunday Sept. 8th 1872

Rose late, about 9. Read papers, cut bits out for scrap book. Did not wash till after dinner. Cleaned boots for Monday. Wrote to Morse. Thought about writing to Beck, put it off till weekday. Bill and I went to Chapel, Jimmy Harcombe sat along with us. Preece preached a poor sermon. Took out Maria for a walk. In at 9 p.m. Practised in *Service* hymn book for about an hour. Off to bed. No prayers.

Monday Sept. 9th 1872

Woke about 5 a.m., dull day. Came on to rain before I got to Trafalgar. Mr. W.B.B. came up in stores, gave instruction concerning patent oil. Cleaned an old lamp for him and tinkered it up according to orders. Wrote Mr. Wood concerning lamp to be repaired and took note myself.

Left at 5.20, rained, pouring all way home, got legs very wet. Took clock to Greenings for repairs. Jewelry not completed for Mrs. W.B.B. Clock to be done and jewelry both together. Bought loaf for C.C.B., lamp on appro. for W.B.B. Parcel for Morgan's at 9.30. Read chapter. Prayers, thought, meditated. Bed 10 p.m.

Tuesday Sept. 10th

Early to work. Took lamp from Woods, parcel from Morgan's, loaf for C.C.B. Took Miss Ellen Preece of Ruardean in pit, lost C.C.B. Went in at 2, out at 5 p.m. Stores left to themselves all afternoon. Kept piece of coal got by Miss Preece. Engaged to go there on Sunday.[73]

Went to practise tonic sol-fa. Had good night, shook hands with Mr. Waites. Maria had letter advising her of situation, going to leave us. Thought of buying writing case for her. To be considered on Saturday. Bed at 10.30 p.m.

Wednesday Sept. 11th 1872

Rose at 5 a.m., at stores early. Worked all day, and [deputised] for Smith at night. Rode home with Cooksey, Landy and others. No fish left. Did not call at Woods for bolts as per order. Prayers and in bed by 2.

Thursday Sept. 12th 1872

Rose late, at work at 6.20. 'Not dead but sleepeth' written on stores door by W.B.B. No letter come today, quite in a concern. Letter not got into proper hands or some reply would have come.

Shops shut, could not get Mosoo's boots. Got bolts from Woods. Wrote Beck. Going to Gloster Saturday, all being well. Very sleepy. Bed at 9 p.m.

Friday

Omitted till Monday night. To be entered up. Worked for Smith at weighing. Error in reckoning up oil account. Told to write to Dr. Evans, Reading. Forget the rest.

Saturday

At work in good time. Pay day, the day appointed for a 10 per cent rise but not recieved. Did not see W.B.B. all day. No Jenkins or Mosooo. Mr. Werner[74] came to [Littledean] Woodside.[75] Invited me to tea at Mosooo's. Would see Misses Preece and John Mason if I went. Changed mind and went to Gloster.

Saw Dick Porter and his wife, told me he was off up fields to have some. Rode up with Harry Tocknell. Got in about 8.40. Saw Morse on platform as soon as we alighted. Supped at Wootton Hill Cottage. Left there, went up in town, spent 2/– for tie (blue one), 1/6 for tame rat, 6d. sweets, 1/2d. for collars, 2/10d. fare both ways, 1½d. for paper. Got to Peter [Loveridge]'s at 12 midnight. Slept comfortable. Took rat to bed. Rat piss'd the bed. Very tired. Slept soundly. 2 quarts ale 1/–.

Total 9/1½d.

Sunday Sept. 15th

Rose about 8.30 a.m. Lighted fire at Peter's, breakfasted, talked and went to Morse's. Rat for Alice[76] not accepted. Took back again. Dined at Peter's, leg of lamb, kidney beans &c. Went out in afternoon down Cheltenham Road, across by Cross Keys, Barnwood, went on to Avenue across fields. Took tea at Peter's, very nice. Enjoyed ourselves very much. Saw Bessie's brother John Mathews. Sat down and talked good while. Peter and he went to Barnwood together. Beck and I sat and kept Bessy company till about 9 p.m. then left for Wootton. Met Peter just beyond assylum. Took supper at Wootton. Left house about 10.30. Squeezed Beck extra hard. Beck's animal spirits and my own much excited. Promised to write soon. Invited Peter to Woodside. Shall get a line on Saturday or perhaps Friday to say. Went by mails after wishing Mrs. and Rowland Morse goodbye. Gave Rowland rat. Goodbye Gloster.

Monday

Rose at 5.40, got to Trafalgar about 6.30. Mr. W.B.B. from home. No letter from [Dr] Evans, Reading. Wrote to him as though written on Friday. Went to Mr. Rhodes to see about letter, found it had been there since 7th and had been opened. Remonstrated quite sharp with Rhodes about it. He pretended to be very sorry and said no one but a William Henry Williams had seen the letter or broken the seal of it.

Brought watch to have glass put in for Smith. Enquired for Mrs. Brain's jewelry and clock. Not done, but will be by Wednesday without fail. Went to Cinderford [Goods] Station at night, enquiring if parcel from Evans had come there, but no. Mr. Long promised to bring parcel from Dr. Evans from

Newnham tomorrow [if there]. Paid Long 2/– for cover of book. Sweets 2/–. Payed McKusky for trowsers 13/–. Bought bottle of port 2/3d. Bed at 11 p.m.

Total 17/5d.

Tuesday Sept. 17th 1872

Worked in stores first turn, in weighbox second turn. Rode home flying in cart, 7 beside. Did nothing beside.

Wednesday Sept. 18th 1872

Rose late. Up at Trafalgar by 6.20. Worked in stores one turn. Wrote deed or document for Great Western Railway today about level crossing[77] and copied agreement.

Home at 5.50 p.m. Tea. To Longs to enquire for parcel. No parcel arrived. Took clock to Greenings. Bought alarm 11/6d. Enquired for jewellry at Greenings, promised by tomorrow faithfully. Received 4d. owed from William Green. Wrote Beck. Practised upon piano. Bed 10.30. John gone first.

Total spent 11/4d.

Thursday Sept. 19th 1872

Rose at 5.30 a.m. At Trafalgar received note from Ellen Preece, for her piece of coal cut Sept. 10th. Wrote line to her, but John Mason was gone before I could send it. Wrapped it up nicely, dated it &c and put ready for morning. Mr. Cordwin's lad found parcel from Dr. Evans at Newnham Station. Sent 1/– carriage, gave Mr. Cordwin 6d. for boy's trouble. Will arrive about 11 a.m. tomorrow.

Cleaned and went out. Took order to Mr. Wood for knifes took previous day. Read *Ross Gazette*, played accordion. Went to corner of Baptist Chapel. Saw Crawshay's coachman and Miss Cooper, milliner from Edwards, down on her back in Chapel Yard, clothes turned well up and going the rig arright. William Green and I watched them down over the green and lost them. To bed at 10.50 p.m.

Total spent 1/6d.

Friday Sept. 20th 1872

Received box from Mr. Cordwin about 10 a.m. at Trafalgar. Worked for Smith at night. Forgot to do diary up till Monday. Got home at 2 a.m.

Saturday Sept. 21st 1872

Rose 6 a.m. To work late. Not much doing. W.B.B. smiled, knowingly. Left about 3.30 p.m. Home, polished walking stick for Joe Jay, bought paper from Mr. Longs for scrap book, paid for *Forester*. Changed *Forester* for *Ross Gazette*. Cut all scraps out of *Budgett*, Mountjoy's speech from *Forester* &c. Received note from Ellen Preece, partly a solicitation for Sunday afternoon. Went out to Woods, bought glass paper for sticks &c. Posted up scrap book. Bed at 10.50 p.m.

'Go no more a-courting to Ruardean.'

Sunday Sept. 22nd 1872

Rose about 9.30 a.m. Read paper, wrote first part of diary over in ink. Dined at 1 p.m. Cleaned and off to Ruardean. People in Church singing *Nunc Dimitis* as I passed. Walked down road toward Walford. Back up, left John Mason's book. Spoke to

Henry Read and Harry Jenkins. Went up road with Harry Jenkins, met the Miss Preeces, invited to tea, promised to meet again about 6 p.m. Met John Mason and lass coming down the lane. Spoke and proposed to meet in half an hour. Henry and I went on top of meadow, took view off stile. Spied the Misses Preece coming up to Chapel, joined them. Mason and Jenkins could not decide on coming along. Went with both to Drybrook School. Heard good sermon by Mr. Barker of Holy Trinity Church. Text, 'If the righteous scarcely be sated, how shall the ungodly and the sinner appear?' Good sermon. Walk'd back with the ladies, took supper with them. Saw the C.D.V.s, knew several. Most comfortable reception. Enjoyed it much. Brought back by Laura and Ellen Preece. Passed by C.C.B., did not get recognized. Took affectionate farewell of both, especially Nellie. Laura going back to Plymouth on Wednesday. Left my stick, given by John Gray, in remembrance of me. Thinking of poor Beck all the time I was jilting her, resolving not continue the practice. Go no more a-courting to Ruardean. Returned home about 12 p.m. at night. Bed. ['Saw a nude' has been deleted.]

Monday Sept. 23rd 1872

Rose at 6 a.m., work by 6.30 a.m. W.B.B. in quite an excited mood over the preparations for new Chapel. Requested to take ticket off Miss Kingscote[78] for Chapel. Declined till another day. Chaffed by C.C.B. about yesterday at Ruardean. Copied out C.C.B.'s letter from his brother Noah. Very busy all the day with lamps &c for Chapel.

Came home about 5.30 p.m. Wash'd, done up diary &c, practised on tonic sol-fa, marking Maria's linen. Bed about 11.30.

Tuesday Sept. 24th 1872

Rose late, broke alarum. Received letter from Ellen Preece to go to opening of Chapel in evening. Mason and Jenkins left at mid-day, went to Ross instead of tea meeting.

Left Trafalgar about 4.20 p.m. Cleaned. Went to Cordwins,

bought book *Enquire Within upon Everything* for Maria 6d., packet of paper. Took ring to Greenings to be re-stoned. Went to Drybrook Chapel about 7 p.m. Saw J. Hurcombe, went in to his sister's shop. Went on to Drybrook, in to Philip Jordans. Paid for 2 glasses hot rum for I and Hurcombe, 8d. Went back to Chapel. People just coming out. Saw Nelly and Laura and Mrs. Bennett of the *Malt Shovel*, Ruardean. Was introduced to her as a friend. Walked home with Ellen, took two glasses beer. Nellie and Laura came back to pike [house] with me. Laura ran home, Nellie stayed with me. Went back again. Couldn't do the amicable Quaker.[79] Took leave of both. Both off on Thursday for Plymouth and Taunton. Promised to answer letter from Nellie as soon as received and to send C.D.V. as soon as could be taken. Got home at 12.30, all abed. Did not see Maria to say goodbye. Must write in a few days. Bed at 1 a.m.

Total spent 3/9d.

Wednesday Sept. 25th 1872

Jenkins and I breakfast together, John Mason off all day marking timber. Miss Kingscote come into stores (weighed 126 lbs). Mrs. Brain wanted me to wait at table on arrival of Mr. Marling, Stroud. Took dinner along with servants. Mrs. Bickerton assisted at waiting. Told her I was at Ellen's when she came to sell tickets for tea party. Work'd for Smith second shift. Received letter from Emily.[80] No sense much. Book'd colliers out of pit. Came home flying in cart.

Thursday Sept. 26th 1872

Woke late, took fish up. Mr. W.B.B. had chalked on the door. Arthur came to me about 11 a.m., said he had left home. Father and him had fallen out. Looking for work. Asked Chapell for a job and offered to put him in the saw mill. Came from the stores about 5 to 5 p.m. Ruth Price and W.B.B. laughing &c. Something suspicious going on in house. Jane remarked that he knew when Mrs. W.B.B. had gone out. Mr. W.B.B. spoke of my nocturnal duties for Smith incapacitating me for morning duty in stores. Was to have brought a hat to be repaired but girls couldn't find out the same. Left it there. Pogson put my accordion up for raffle at 50/–. Could not go to Greenings or Woods, shops shut.

Arthur came home and slept with me. Bed at 10 p.m.

Friday September 27th 1872

Stores all day. Took up accordion to be raffled for. Pogson took job in hand. Mr. W.B.B. tried it, liked it very much. Went to Cinderford to post office for licence for crest and to ascertain schedule of charges for crest on paper &c. To Greenings for alarum, &c. Called at home and took supper and told inmates not to wait up. Went to Trafalgar, weighed for Smith. Slept in stores. Up in time in morning. Pay due Saturday.

Saturday Sept. 28th 1872

Pay. Took £2/3/3 and £2/10/– for the instrument won by C. Cotton by a 41 shake. Received £5/13/3 for pay and accordion. Sent off 3£ for concertina by Pogson. Rode home in cart with Mossoo. Went to Dick's for pair of boots. Bought pair of slippers 3/6d. Wrote Maria. Coppied out letter for Ellen Preece. Read little, and bed.

	£	s	d
Total spent	£3	3	6
Mrs. Green's bill	1	17	8
	5	1	2
Bottle of rum		2	2
	5	3	4

Sunday

Rose late. Stopped in house. Did nothing all day. Cleaned. Stringer waiting to accompany me to Chapel. Would not go. Went to Chapel late. Preece preached, did not hear what about or where from.

'Went to Chapel late.' *Cinderford Baptist Chapel.*

Monday Sept. 30th 1872

Stormy, foggy morning. Full day. Stores all day. Jenkins and Mr. Walter off at Newnham. John Mason alone. C.C.B. had friends, conducting them round works. Wrote a letter to Ellen Preece. No letter from Beck. Bought two basins 5d., two books 1/6d. Took clock to Greenings for repairs. Took licence out for W.B.B.'s crest. Gave Annie Tyndale ½d. for fireworks. Cut out scraps from papers. Bed 11.30.

Total spent 1/11½d.

Tuesday Oct. 1st 1872

Rose late, up by 6.10 at Trafalgar. No letter from Beck. Wrote Ellen Preece at Willeton [Somerset]. Learned lesson off Pogson in *New System of Instrument*. Wrote Arthur. Calculated Chapell's cash, £6/1/4½d. Rode down on engine.

Home about 6 p.m. Took Mr. W.B.B.'s licence for Crest. Order'd boots for J. Conolly[81] on appro. Went to singing class. T. Rhodes[82] gave exercise on modulator, Mr. Waites on lessons and lecture. Two new tunes. Took Bessy Tingle home, very nearly did the Amiable Quaker for her. Left her 10 p.m. Saw two down in the lane hard at it. Wrote to try and get rid of Nellie Preece telling her to look above colliers &c. Look'd out for Bessy Cooper. No chance. Bed at 11 p.m.

Wednesday Oct. 2nd 1872

Worked second turn for Smith. Book'd out colliers. Took boots for Conolly, one pair suited. Rode home flying. Home by 1.30 a.m. No letter from any one. Stormy day. Bed at 1.50 a.m.

Thursday Oct. 3rd 1872

Heard alarum and dropt asleep again. Woke at 6 a.m., at Trafalgar by 6.20 a.m. Took fish. Men waiting. Forgot C.C.B.'s lamp, told him it was broken. C.C.B. quite pert[83] about his lamp. Pogson received postcard from London about concertina. No letter today. Wrote Beck a sneerer. Wrote piece out of *Gloster Journal* for scrap book, and *Ross Gazette* as well.

Home by 5.50. Practised tonic sol-fa, posted up diary. Bought and paid for hand lamp for self 2/6d., stamp 1d. C.C.B.'s lamp got broken, glass 4d. to be put in. Total spent 3/–.

Very stormy day. Bill and I in parlour. Dobbs, Jim, two girls, John and Stringer all in kitchin. Like bedlim with brass instruments and other rows. Practice night for boys. Mrs. Green brewed this day.

Friday Oct. 4th 1872

Work at 5.45 a.m. Morning wet, day miserable. No letter from anywhere. Worked for Smith. Came home flying in cart. Two carts down together, about 10 of us. Did not go to bed. Had two or three cups of rum and tea. Kept lamp burning, slept on floor by fire till 5 a.m. Got up, washed and off to work at 5.15. There before 6 a.m.

Saturday 5–10–1872

Morning wet and inclement. Did scarcely anything all day. Left at 3 p.m. Brought parcel for Mrs. Cook where Bessie Cooper lives, one from Charlotte Cooksey for her mother to be left at Tom Gardiner's, and a message from Mrs. Brain to Mrs. R. Barnets near Haywood. Orders from C.C.B. for clock &c and from Mr. Walter to call for his paper. Met Mrs. Jones of the lodge, she had brought it.

Home about 4 p.m. Wrote Beck. Did not go out. Nothing but reading. Received nasty letter from the old woman at Gloster.[84] Bed at 10 p.m. Papers 5d., stamp 1d.

6d. altogether

Sunday Oct. 6th 1872

Rose at 10 a.m. Breakfast, read, talked, dined, tonic'd half hour, cleaned, slept, tea and Chapel. Went to Haywood with Charlie Ashley. Went to Steam Mills with Bessy and Mira Cooper. Brought them home. Romp'd. Felt tuzymuzy indoors. Supp'd, talked half hour to landlady. Posted up diary from Thursday. No prayers, no bible. Bed 11.30.

Monday Oct. 7th 1872

Rose at 5.40 a.m. At work by 6.20. Dull morn, Chappel opening the ball on pit men and pumpers. Nothing passing in day of any importance. John Mason went to Parkhend with timber hauliers. C.C.B. turned up, dress'd in new coat with seal skin collar and cuffs. Off in Mr. W.B.B.'s trap – who but he! Spoke to Mrs. W.B.B. on leaving work. Mr. W.B.B., Mossoo, Frank Chivers and Albert Mason went down in pit dialing &c[85] about 4.10 p.m.

Left work at 5 precisely. Brought bit of glue and bit of solder. Borrow'd can for glue. Brought up Mrs. Brain's jewellry from

'C.C.B. turned up, dressed in new coat with seal skin collar and cuffs – who but he!'

Greenings. Chatted a bit. Called at Bouds. Was informed Lloyd had left and gone to Coleford. Promised to buy lamp from there on Saturday next. Bought cup with *Dickens* on 4d., paper $1\frac{1}{2}$d., pipe stem 1d. Ordered two quires exercise paper from Cordwins for phonography. Going to take fresh start. Could not recollect where to take the hat to. Home, took cucumber for supper. Posted up diary. Bed at 10.30 p.m. Mrs. Green baked.

Tuesday October 8th 1872

Up at 5.20 a.m., at Trafalgar at 6.10 a.m. Posted up four days in day book. Apprized of the arrival of my instrument. Pogson rose late and did not bring it up. Took up Mrs. W.B.B.'s jewellry. Delivered to Charlotte through window in morning about 7 a.m. Gypsies came at dinner time and went into front of garden and talked to family through bedroom window. Came back by stores. John Mason tried to do amiable Quaker. Did not catch them. Gave orders for stores. Mr. Little called in afternoon to see how standing for offal. Told him to come early part of next week. Left about 5.10, put tallow for Alf Roberts after 5 p.m. Lost key of door.

Came home just before 6 p.m. Letter from Maria had been opened. Very much put out about it. Threw it bang in fire as soon as discovered. Wouldn't hear a word of excuse. Wrote and told Maria all about it. Sent *Forester* and music book. Practice at tonic sol-fa. Went to a Mrs. Cooks by furnace, formerly Miss Withington from Wilkes, with hat for Mrs. Brain. Came to bed at 10.30 p.m.

4d. spent

Wednesday October 9th 1872

Stores by day, weighed at night (beautiful black discourses). Recieved concertina from Dan Pogson. Tried it at night, good one. Had 2 quarts of beer, 8d., in weighbox. Home with more in cart, played going home. No letter.

Spent 8d.

Thursday Oct. 10th 1872

In stores, work'd one turn. Pit played second turn. Mr. W.B.B. out on horseback. Mr. C.C.B. ordered me to go and fetch fish that was not sent to my lodgings. Refused to go. C.C.B. gone out with Conolly in trap. Sent for cocoa. Did not get it. Gave girl 2d. for going.

Home. Walked very hard (coming to rain), Morris and Aaron Weaver keeping up. Three letters waiting, one from Beck, one from Ellen Preece, the other from somebody at Newent to apply for a girl's character. Not for me. Opened and sealed it up again. Practised on concertina, Bill along, in parlour. Mrs. Green not speaking to me owing to Maria's letter. Went to bed at 10.30 p.m.

2d. spent

Friday morning Oct. 11th 1872

Morning very rough. Rose at 5.40, late 10 minutes. Brought paper from Kitsill for Mr. Walter. Received letter from Maria Green instead of one burned. Read scraps concerning Mason, Jenkins, and C.C.B. from Nellie's letter. John Mason received a letter from Dr. Evans of Reading requesting payment of bill for antiseptic medicine and advice. Read in *Gloucester Journal* of the death of Mr. Kiddle's wife, Rose Anne, and also the death of the Revd. Armitage of St. Luke's vicarage.[86] Poor Morse must feel it. Will write him if there's time today. Wrote Beck and Nellie. Smith had Beck's likeness, showed it to me. Sent Lerigo for powder in the morning. Ruth showed me my likeness with wig on. Promised to exchange for another one. Smith working out of his turn in my place.

Undecided about going to Gloster on Sunday. Bought two candles 4d., paper 1½d., three stamps 3½d. Spent 3d. for Austin's air gun. Mrs. Green a little more familiar today. Practised on instrument two hours. Read a chapter. Bed at 10 p.m.

Spent 11d. today

Oct. 12th 1872

Saturday, Rough wind in morning. Rose at 5.20 a.m., up at Trafalgar by 6 a.m. Took Austin's air gun. Mr. Walter delighted. Before breakfast paid petty cash out of own pocket 1/6d., could not make it meet. Bensir's representative called. Ask'd if I was Mr. Williams, said he came upon that oil that was sent back. Catechised me. I referred him to engine men about it. Pay today. Wages £2/3/3. Received from Smith 16/–, 8d. owing.

Rode home with several. Bought papers 2d. and paid for 2 glasses of ale for Jarrett and self at Darringtons. Shot three shots each at Beard's gallery. Jarrett had to pay. Bought Mosooo 2 oz. of tobacco from Cordwins and paid for my paper 2/–. Spoke to

Wordsworth, cheap jack. Said he had a good fair at Ross. Paid Bill Green a borrowed penny. Washed and cleaned boots, practised shorthand two hours, concertina &c, posted up diary. Supped on two fresh herrings. Paid bill &c. Spent £1/5/9.

	£ s. d.
Fortnight's pay Received	2 19 11
Spent	2 3
Bill	1 3 6
In hand	1 14 2

Sunday Oct. 13th. 1872

Rose at 8 a.m., played concertina, cut scraps, read papers &c. Dined at 1 p.m., lamb, apple pie &c. Started at 1.50 for 3 p.m. train to Gloucester. Disappointed, no train till 5.45 p.m. Stayed at Kings. Drank four glasses of beer. Paid for police[man] and King two glasses 9d. Tickets to and fro 1/10d., Poldens musk drops 3d. Gave child 1½d. Train half hour late, got in Gloster at 6.45.

At Wootton by 7 p.m. Beck at St. Catherine's Church. Met her beyond Court of Probate coming out. Drank two glasses ale at Wootton. Had severe lecture from Beck. Passed off very well. Ask'd poor Beck when it was to be. Said she didn't know and ran away. Told me Mrs. Robert's grievance. Sorely put out because I did not put up there. Left between 10 and 11 p.m. Wished good bye.

Came to the station. Stayed in parcel office some time. Row on platform. Gave little Turner my stick for a present. Spoke to Tom Hacker on platform. Did not go to Morse's, the first time I missed calling since I left there. Mission to Gloster was to hear the funeral sermon of the Revd. Armitage but it was preached the previous Sunday by the Bishop and Canon Harvey. Disappointed quite. Came to Newnham by mails. Did not see anyone to give up ticket to. Brought it home. On coming up first meadow found myself accompanied by a beautiful black spaniel dog. Followed me home. Fed him.

THE LATE REV. G. ARMITAGE.

St. Luke's Church was on Sunday morning last crowded by a large and sympathetic congregation, most of whom were attired in mourning, to hear Bishop Ellicott preach the funeral sermon on the late Rev. G. Armitage. The service throughout was of a most devotional character, and during the sermon many of the congregation were much affected. The prayers and lessons were read by the Rev. J. V. Payne, and the Rev. Canon Lysons.

The Bishop took for his text the 13th verse of the 14th chapter of the Book of Revelations: "Blessed are the dead which die in the Lord from henceforth: yea, saith the Spirit, that they may rest from their labours; and their works do follow them." In commencing, his lordship said he had come among them during this very sorrowful season in part by the promptings of his own heart, and in the next place because he thought it might be in some degree a comfort to them if he spoke a few words of commemoration and of general consolation. And so he had come, sorrowfully enough, God knew, and yet at the same time with that deep thankfulness of heart that ought to possess all when they turned their thoughts to the general course of him whom it would be his duty especially to commemorate that day. Their true and faithful pastor was now in rest, and nearer to that Lord and Master whom he had served so faithfully and so well. No text that he could have chosen could really have been more suitable in reference to their dear departed friend. It spoke of a rest after death, after the care and turmoil of this world. No more sin, no more temptation, no more divided feelings in the minds of the very best of men; nothing but rest, peace, and greater nearness to the Lord. Then the words "Their works do follow them," were so suitable. The life of their dear friend, as they all knew, was one of faithfulness and usefulness. It seemed but a little time ago since he (the Bishop) came at Mr. Armitage's special desire to that church, when arrangements were made for enlarged accommodation, and on this occasion he desired to recognize the earnest christian work done in that House of God. And then when they thought of the works done amongst them, when they passed those noble schools, a monument of his quiet, persevering faithfulness, they could not but feel that a spirit of earnestness marked their dear pastor. Of his faithfulness in preaching it was not necessary to say much.

'Mission to Gloster was to hear the funeral sermon of the Revd Armitage.' Gloucester Journal, *12 October 1872*

Monday Oct. 14th 1872

Rose about 5.30, up at work at 6.10 a.m. Dog went out with Bill in the morning, came back at night. Pit played both turns – Ruardean feast and Littledean's Hill fair (Micklemas). Worked posting up book &c. Wrote for corn.[87]

Took Boud's order for cans. Bought lamp 4/3d., pepper box 1d., tin can 5d., oil 3½d., total 5/0½d. Practised concertina short time. Pritchard and wife at Mrs. Green's, Pritchard trying concertina. Saw Mr. Walter at Cinderford and enquired about Jenkins and Mason. He told me they had started for the fair. Mr. W.B.B. and family (or part) drove by at about 9 p.m. whilst in at Bouds. Listened to cheap jack a short time. Home, lit lamp, wrote phonography for a quarter of an hour. Fed dog, brought him downstairs, let him run out for air. Back, put bed for him. To bed. Prayers in bed.

Tuesday Oct. 15th 1872

Woke at 5.45 a.m. Brought dog for Mr. W.B.B., told Mr. Walter his history, gave him in Mr. Walter's care. Was advised to advertize him. Forgot two parcels left by Morgans. Mr. Osbald Diston, Birmingham, called to solicit orders. Took order for files. Presented me with 2/–, told me to write to them at any time I wanted anything. Paid Dan Pogson 15/– for accordion, 1/– for carriage order &c. Asked him to speak to James Baldwin as I intended to buy harmonium instead.

Left work at 5.10 p.m., home at 6 p.m. Gave Jenkins a note for Beck. Wrote to her as soon as I went home. Practised on shorthand half an hour, concertina one hour. Went to class, tonic sol-fa. Miss Ridgely back behind listening to progress of new choir. Made her laugh whilst singing her part of the *Messiah*. Broke up at 9.30 p.m. Stayed half an hour after to listen to Miss Ridgley and Messrs. Edwards and Waites. Bowed to Miss Ridgley, acknowledged and returned, when leaving. Bought ticket of admission to the Choral Union[88] off Bessie Tingle 1/–. Home, supped. Bed at 11.40 p.m. Thought when knives and forks are wanted to write to <u>Louis Osbald Diston, Sheffield</u>.

Wednesday October 16th 1872

Rose at 5.10 a.m. Came on to rain, pouring. Quite dark till 6 a.m. Up at Trafalgar when the whistle blew. Took two parcels from Morgans for W.B.B. House occupants up preparing breakfast for Mr. Walter and W.B.B. Both off to Gloucester by 7 a.m. Phelp's case on, and the watch case as well.[89]

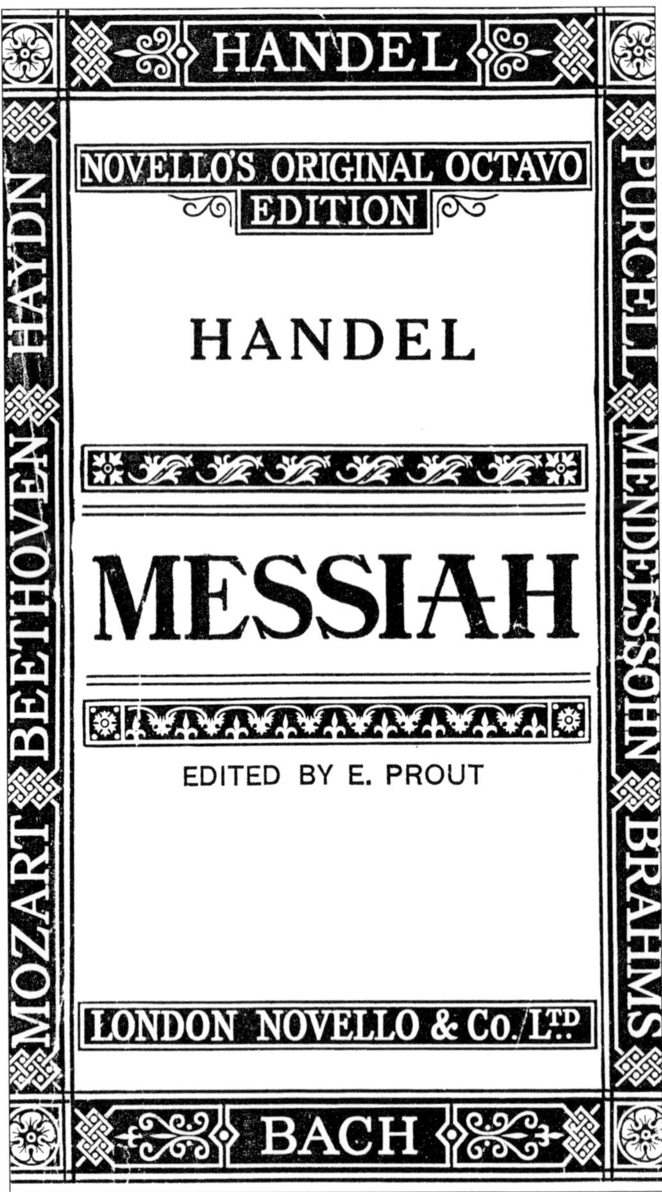
HANDEL
NOVELLO'S ORIGINAL OCTAVO EDITION
HANDEL
MESSIAH
EDITED BY E. PROUT
LONDON NOVELLO & Co. LTD
BACH
MOZART BEETHOVEN HAYDN
PURCELL MENDELSSOHN BRAHMS

'Made Miss Ridgley laugh whilst singing her part of the *Messiah*.'

Spent some time up in upper office with Johnny Mason talking matters over, talking business &c. John says he has kept his diary 2 years and over: Lesson for William Henry Williams. Went to the office for John Mason to show me how to draw up an aggreement. John sent away his paper to Bristol. I helped him secure the bags &c. Booked men out. Ask'd to take note for Charlotte. Refused. Not going home.

Left stores at 5 p.m. Weighed (night turn). Have not noticed James Brain anywhere all night up to 9 p.m. Ben Bennett weighed with me, or rather chequed my weight in weighbox. Went down for water for coffee. Brought coffee instead of cocoa this day. Mason and I took some for dinner. Jenkins is at Gloster. He took note for Beck. Anxious to learn result. Kear talking about Warry says he doesn't keep men to do nothing. Fatter than himself. Book'd men out of pit at 11.30 p.m., Hodge's company last. Mr. William B. Brain came home at night. Mr. Walter and Jenkins stayed at Gloster.

Rode home in cart. Went like wildfire. About ten or twelve of us. Self boiled two eggs for supper. Bed about 2 a.m. Left lamp burning by the alarum all the morning.

Thursday Oct. 17th 1872

Rose at 5.30 a.m., at Trafalgar by 6.10 a.m. Moonlight. Took fish from Morgan's. Frank Brain spoke about the tea and Choral Union at Cinderford. Intend being present. Charlotte refused to shake hands this morn. Expect gave offence by refusing to take note last night for a Mrs. Gardner. Mason went to Gloster. I ask'd Jane if going to Choral Union. Reply negative. Traveller for S. Heeley & Co., Birmingham, here at dinner time. Mr. W.B.B. wanted to know if storekeeper hadn't account of tiles then going away to T.B.B.'s farm. Self ask'd leave to go to Choral Union. Granted.

Left Trafalgar at 4.10 p.m. Ran nearly all the way down line. Overtook Mason at the tip, walk'd up to Woodside with him. Overtook Polly Dykins at top of hill, wished her a good evening. Compliment returned. Passed by Mr. Marfell going to tea. Promised to be there in a quarter of an hour after. Went home, changed and went to the Chapel. Tea had commenced, couldn't procure seat. Went home to tea. Returned in a quarter of an hour to Chapel. Tea nearly over. Had two bits of cake and two cups of tea. Shook hands with Miss Simms from Waites's and Bessie

Cooper from Edwards'. Bill Green, D. Clark, Amos Tingle, Charlie Ashley of our class waiting on congregation. Went up into gallery, procured capital seat. Chapel crammed to excess. Mr. Preece addressed audience and opened service. Mr. Tetley presided and lectured on the tunes that were selected for the festival, showing their origin and their power, their meaning and beauty, their adaptiveness &c. Sublime music and selections. Choirs from Lydbrook, Coleford, Chepstow, Monmouth.

Singing broke up at 9.30 p.m. C.C.B. standing at Chapel gates. Passed him by, didn't speak. Home at 9.35. Discussed on the festival &c. To bed at 10.40.

Friday Oct. 18th 1872

Shied up at 5.50. Heavy rain fell in the night. Found stores door wide open. Left open all night. Jenkins and Mr. Walter came home last night from Gloster. Baker, Phelps and Henry Morgan get a month, the watch case [James Whitson] comes off free. Mason in Gloster yesterday, met Miss Ford and ran against Jenkins and Mr. Walter there. Saw Jenkins, said he did not take my note to Wootton Hill Cottage.

John Mason did not come to stores to breakfast. Jenkins and I fed together. Mr. W.B.B. off in carriage about 9.20. Mr. Werner came up in stores, talked a bit. Tom Jayne put an hour up in stores. Left stores at 5 p.m. [In office] wrote to F. & P. [Fielding & Pratt], Gloster, for Burrows for fly wheel. Sent note to Cordwins by Burrows. Weighed for Smith second turn, only 3 turns due from Smith and 8d. from last time, 10/8d.

Home in cart flying, 11 of us. Jim up at 2 a.m. Left lamp burning by clock, put alarum to go down at 4 a.m. Bed at 2.10 a.m.

Saturday October 19th 1872

Shied up at 6 a.m. Up at Trafalgar by 6.30 a.m., all of a sweat. Took Mr. Walter an account of 20 trusses of hay received last night about 6.30 p.m. from Mr. Mansell of Mitcheldean which were not weighed at Strip,[90] man gone home. Smith in weighbox ill, got jaw ache and wife breeding. Received from Bouds six half

THURSDAY.

Both Courts sat this morning, and disposed of the following cases :—

William Prowse, 14, labourer, to 14 days' imprisonment, and five years' detention at Hardwicke Reformatory, for stealing a watch from W. Warner, at St. George's.

George Rogers, 19, collier, to three months, for feloniously receiving a watch, the property of W. Warner

William Baker, 32, labourer, to six months, for maliciously wounding Eliza Carter, at St. George's.

Charles Cook, 27, woodman, to two years, and five years' police supervision, for stealing a hand-cart from the Rev. John Constable, and a plough and iron wheel from Russell Swanwick, at Cirencester.

George Young, 17, and George Browne, 16, labourers, to one month each, for burglary at Stroud.

Thomas Phelps and Henry Morgan, to one month, for stealing 3 tons 13 cwt. of coal from Messrs. Brain, at East Dean.

Mary Ann Tudor, 17, servant, for burglary at Frocester, to ten days.

William James, 34, labourer, seven years' penal servitude, for stealing potatoes from Charles Pullen and Mary Adams, at Marshfield.

William Meek, seven years' penal servitude, for stealing pork at East Dean.

Elizabeth Wakefield to one month, for stealing a petticoat and an axe, the property of Henry Shelswell, at Weston-on-Avon.

The following were acquitted :—

George Farmer and George Watts, charged with stealing mutton at Cheltenham.

James Whitson, charged with stealing a watch from W. B. Brain, at East Dean.

Mark Maggs, 26, labourer, charged with maliciously wounding Richard Field at Winterbourne.

'Baker, Phelps and Henry Morgan get a month, the watch case comes off free.' Gloucester Journal, *19 October 1872.*

gallon cans and six gallon ditto, and was informed that my cup was come. To call for it tonight and change globe of lamp. Mr. W.B.B. took his lamp, and Burrows and him gone into pit. Water up and trying to remedy it.[91]

Left Trafalgar 2 p.m. Took lamp globe to Bouds to exchange. Recieved cup with frog in bottom for a present. Hung it up with one of *Charles Dickens*. Home at 4 p.m. Spent nothing on Saturday. To bed at 11 p.m. Prayers in bed.

Sunday Oct. 20th 1872

Rose at 10.30 a.m., too late for Chapel. Cleaned at 11 a.m., dined, beef and plum pudding. Avott[92] called for me about 3 p.m., took me to his house, gave me a beautiful pear, show'd me harmonium. Tried it and stayed to tea. Came to Chapel together. Self sat in gallery along with William Green. Went straight home, supped and to bed.

Monday Oct. 21st 1872

Mullock'd out at 6 a.m., at Trafalgar at 6.30 a.m. Very wet and disagreeable all day. Wrote John Miller and Beck. Sent Miller 10/– for Club [Oddfellows Society] and promised 2/– next week for Chapel. Mr. W.B.B. called for his lamp early, i.e. 10 a.m., and went in pit. Took telegram[93] from W.B.B. for Burrows to come down at once. Went out and found Burrows. Called John Morris in stores and asked him to make me a foot iron for nailing boots &c. Received letter from Beck telling me she dreamed that I was in prison. Thought of what I had asked of I. Morgan.[94] Stop it tomorrow.

No shorthand tonight. Bought lamp chimney 4d. for Ben Bennett and 6d. stamp for self, and brush 6d. for chimney of own lamp.

Beautiful letter, quite melting, from poor old Morse. I thought how nice to have a friend like Morse to write to. Mrs. Green had nice supper, pig meat &c, ready, and sago pudding. Read Beck's letter several times. Sent Morse's to Beck. Posted up diary. A man come from Littledean to buy the wig on condition his wife approves of it. Will call on Thursday when I am at home. Received £1 for it. Read 14th of *St. John*. Prayers and meditation, bed 11 p.m.

1/– spent

Tuesday Oct. 22 1872

Rolled out at 4 a.m., beautiful moonlight morning. Look'd at clock, turned in again till 5 a.m. Up at 5, at Trafalgar at 5.40 a.m. Thinking of Beck's dream, told Johnny Mason about it. Mr. W.B.B. called for his lamp after breakfast. Said it worked bad last evening. Mr. Walter up talking to him at same time. Mr. W.B.B. said, 'There's a woman, Wal.' Wal runs off singing out, 'Where?'

Mr. Walter came after breakfast and look'd books over in

stores. Mr. C.C.B. looking very foppish this morning. Told Jim Brain about Beck's dream. Can trust poor Jim. He says inform Chapell and buy the iron off him for foot iron. Done so. Mr. Walter inspecting stores. One cask olive oil short, one cask seal ditto. One bag waste he could not find out the entry thereof. Spoke to Mr. W.B.B. Orders to remind him of cheque for £1/1/– for Rhodes for armorial bearings and to tell Greening to send home all the clocks at once. Received three dozen shovels this day from Norris, Stourbridge.

Left Trafalgar at 5.40 p.m., home at 6 p.m. Received letter from Miss Preece, Willeton. Played concertina short time. Bill informed me that the dog belonged to Mr. Goold, Newnham. Quite alarmed about it.[95]

Received boots, new soled, from Nobbs. To pay. Sent Morse's letter. Stamp 2d. Paid Rhodes for the licence, apologised for not having done so before. Went to singing class. Received good lesson from Mr. Waites on the tonic sol-fa. Discussed the Choral Union over.

Thought good on course to pursue with Nellie Preece. Thought of Beck's sister, and not much chance. Prayers at 11 p.m. Bed 11.15.

4/2d. spent

Wednesday Oct. 23rd 1872

Roll'd out 5.30, at Trafalgar at 6.20. Told Mr. Walter news about the dog. Johnny Mason puzl'd at breakfast time with the word 'popp'd' in Ellen Preece's letter. Beck's dream something like come out. Mr. Walter promised to bear all responsibility respecting dog. I think it a good way to get the dog returned. Took minutes[96] of 2 tons 11 cwt. 1 qr. 21 lb. of iron after breakfast. Observed Samuel Davis, the new Deputy Chief Lieutenant for the colliery, looking over the mound there, blowing his tobacco and waiting about for W.B.B., who appears to be in capital [humour] this morning. Mr. T.B.B. in upper office.

Haviland wanting corn, not a bit in stores. Received corn at dinner time. Samuel Davis and Dan Pogson holding confab in stores. Samuel Davis taking observations of stores, talked a little. Mr. Jones there exhibiting horse to Mr. W.B.B. Just spoke and enquired about all at home. Shook hands and off. Saw him again coming from stables.

Smith wanted to work Friday night. I said not so. I want the coin. Informed me pit would play tomorrow and tomorrow night. Tom Fisher promised to write two tunes for me. Weigh'd for Smith tonight.

Took paper to write to Nellie Preece. Going to give the straight griffin[97]: she is too late for the main thing. Did not find time. Book'd men out of pit. Home by 2 a.m. Walk'd, all others gone before. Bed at 2.30 a.m.

Thursday October 24th 1872

Rolled up about 5.45, Trafalgar at 6.15. Took fish. Very dismal and rough, and raining violently all the morn. Mr. W.B.B. up in stores before breakfast. Discovered fish, said he couldn't eat it raw. Orders to call at Woods, Greenings and Bouds to enquire for lamp from Birmingham from Woods and to get Boud to make some of the same sort of lamp as mine and enquire their price. Pit played both turns.

Home at 6 p.m. Alone, no company at home. Mrs. Green baked. Letter from J. Miller. Learned first lesson on piano. Agreed to pay 5/– at quarter's end if Bill learned me the same as himself off the master. Mrs. Green objected to my writing in the parlour. Went to bed. Read the 16th Chap. of *St. John*, the one Morse said was Mr Armitage's favourite. Wrote nothing at home. Bed at 9.30 p.m. Prayers tonight.

Friday Oct. 25th

Shied up at 5.40, at Trafalgar about 6.10 a.m. Served in stores till breakfast. Brought Pogson my last week's *Budget*. Delivered up petty cash in office. Johnny Mason said someone was expected for the dog. John Mason took his bag and gone to Strip [-and-at-it pit] at 12 p.m. Mr. W.B.B. not about work all day. Dan Pogson gave me account of a man, Charles Roberts, who had left the work without giving in his tools. Amount for tools was £2/10/3, coin forthcoming 18/–.

Working for Smith tonight. Tom Fisher brought the tunes *Sing a hymn to Jesus* and *E'er I sleep*. Ben Bennett and I rehearsed them in weighbox. Mr. & Mrs. W.B.B., Mr. Walter and Chappell off at Mrs. Brain's funeral. Came on to rain at night, rain'd incessant. Jarrett away. Had 3 gallons beer from Briarley. Book'd men out of pit.

Came out at 12.40 a.m., rode home in cart, went like lightning. Down at Bilson in about four minutes, one mile and half. Had supper by fire. In bed at 2 a.m.

'John Mason took his bag and gone to Strip.' *Strip-and-at-it Colliery.*

Saturday Oct. 26th 1872

Shied up at 5.45 a.m., down and off in 3 minutes. Ran most of way, at stores in about 20 minutes. Mr. Walter came in stores and told me that Alf Goold Esq. had indicted me for dog stealing, but he was going to send me to his home with the dog and also to send my character &c. Mr. Walter gave me Alf Goold's letter after dinner.

Was given small spanner for banjoe by gas man. While eating breakfast tooth No. 1 broke off and came out. Bought 6 dozen besoms. Received in stores one ton bran, one ton 10 cwt. sharps[98] and 10 sacks oats. Pay received £2/14/2, one day (i.e. night) turn short.

Left work at 4 p.m., home by 5 p.m. Cleaned and started to Newnham at 6.40 p.m. Took dog to Captain Goold's. Got swilled nearly away, rewarded for trouble with nothing. Mr Goold sent note by me to Mr. W.B.B. to thank him (I suppose). Discovered <u>that</u> at Gloster where I went. Saw Beck about 8.30 p.m., quite surprised. Spent till 11 p.m. with her.

Met Cox coming home from London, show'd me his patent lamp. Went on down to station. Saw J. Long. Said he had been head guard three months on Midland Railway. Paid for three quarts ale 1/6d., three pies 9d. Reuben and Auty Brown took share. Old Hornimer too late. Gave him 6d. to have a glass himself. Saw Morse, promised to write, told him my mission.

Rode home with commercial [traveller] from Carmarthen and female from Beanham's Coffee House, Paddington. Had sup of gin out of her bottle. Nearly did the amiable. Her brother and his butty[99] met her. Both drunk, both sore blackguards. Home by 2.30, bed by 3 a.m. Fare to and fro 1/10d.

Spent 4/7d.

Sunday Oct. 27th 1872

Shied up at 1 p.m., breakfast off roast mutton, vegetables and apple pie and pudding. Did not clean till 4 p.m. Clarke, Ashley and another joined in with Bill singing out of *Golden Chain* book. Mrs. Green treated us all with glass of rum and water after dinner. Went to Chapel at night. Minister from Wesleyan Chapel, vapouring with his hands 250 times in 5 minutes or 3120 times per hour. Took note of it. Sent Oliver with two half penny stamps to Newnham to post Captain Goold's letter to W.B.B. Oliver 8d., 4 stamps 2d. No reading. No prayers.

Spent 10d.

Monday Oct. 28th 1872

Rolled out at 6 a.m., at Trafalgar at 6.40 a.m. Beautiful day. Forgot Charlotte's parcel. At dinnertime Mr. C.C.B. came and sent me after naptha lamp for General Woosnam of Bicknor Court. Three ladies and one gent to go down pit. Mr. W.B.B. went down with them, and C.C.B. and Chappell. Emptied both oil casks (vegetable) that I tapp'd and turned out of stores. Going to tap three from Pritchard of Bristol. Cut some leather scraps, three quarters of a pound, for tapping and heeling boots, 6d. Sent post office order for 17/9d. for Mossooo to Samuel Bros., London. Bought 2/– of stamps for John Miller and 6d. for myself, 1d. of blacking from cheap jack, watch from Greening £3/8/–, No. 20892, horizontal seal £1/1/–. Took lamp to Bouds for pattern, bought 3d. card for John Mason. Call'd at Woods for lamps &c. To call next evening. Cleaned and stained 2 gun stocks for Tom Jayne. Sent Beck *Forester*. Practised tonic sol-fa with William Green. Bed at 12 midnight.

Spent £3/0/9d.

Tuesday October 29th 1872

Shied up at 5.30, Trafalgar at 6.10 a.m. Saw Mr. Walter about Captain Goold, told about the dog. Gathered up the old sacks to send to Gloster for corn. Mended up several and filled them ready for the tip. Left work at 5 p.m. Received letter from Beck. Went to practice. Learned good lesson at class. Bed at 12 midnight.

Wednesday October 30th 1872

No posting, all going sorely behind. Received note from C.C. Brain telling me the horses were losing flesh and wanting to know what allowance the horses got to eat now. Did not answer his note. Left Trafalgar about 5 p.m., did not give Mr. W.B.B. his tally paper. No fish came for Trafalgar. Took glass of rum and water at Mrs. Green's expense. Bed at 11 p.m.

Thursday October 31st 1872

Rolled up at 5.30 a.m., at Trafalgar by 6.10 a.m. Mr. W.B.B. and

Mrs. gone with Miss Kingscote to Bristol. Was not at home all day. C.C.B. cutting about sharp. Took Mr. Walter a sample of crushed oats from Mr. E. Little. Proved to be inferior. C.C.B. examined oats that Little ground the other from. Sent sack to Steam Mill to be tested against E. Little's weight of oats. One cwt. 1 quarter 14 lb. before crushed. After, 1 cwt. 1 quarter 6 lb. Traveller from D. Phillips in afternoon. Did not want anything today. Went down to house with W.B.B.'s paper. Had a lark with girls. Ruth accused me of being married. Kept up the game. Pit playing today and yesterday.

Wrote Beck and John Miller. Posted them tonight. Practised on pianno. Bill and Jim gone to practise. Mrs. Green's brother come from Mitcheldean. Bed at 11 p.m.

'Went down to house. Had a lark with girls.' *Trafalgar House, the home of W.B. Brain and his family. The tramway along which Bill Williams rode home runs in front of the house. The upper office is on the extreme left.*

Friday Nov. 1st 1872

Shied up at 5.20, at Trafalgar by 6.20 a.m. Awfully rough and violent winds all night. Very rough and dull in morning. Turned out beautiful day. Saw C.C.B. riding up by gate, legs as stiff as two crutches. Work going on all right again. Received goods in stores from Henry Winfield, Gloster (cowhair and canvas). Had foot iron off John Morris. Gave him 6d. for his work (which was not satisfactory). 2¾ lb. of iron. Paid Chapel 6d. Paid 3d. for Johnny Mason's card. Believed to have paid him before. Was not sure, paid him again.

Left Trafalgar at 5 p.m. Took cheque, &c, for Cordwin. Bought book *Identification of British Nation, Being the Lost Tribes of Israel*, for Mr. Walter, and *Flashes of Light* 4d., and tool book for the firm 3/–. Ordered bespoke pair of boots off Nobbs and paid 3/3d. for taping[100] Wellingtons.

Home soon. Practised on piano, William Green and self. Call'd at Greenings for clocks. None done. Promised to send them round to lodgings. Failed. Had sausages for supper. Bed at 10.10 p.m.

Saturday Nov. 2nd 1872

Shied up at 5.15 a.m., at work at 6.10. Received waste, 2" and 1½" nails, spun, yarn, hemp, tartwire and lamp cotton. Fine morn, wet and stormy. W.B.B. in upper office holding confab with Pogson and Mosoooooo. Took up account of stores received to John Mason. Brought pamphlett for Mr. Walter. Paid 3½d. for it. Promised to bring my *Flashes of Light* and second part of pamphlett for him. Posted up a little.

Left off work at 3.20 p.m. Went home with J. Lander. Rained, pouring. Had lark with gipsies. Mrs. Green's brother at home still. Practised piano and concertina. Bought Lizzie two buns for tea. Did not go out. Bed at 11.10 p.m.

Sunday Nov. 3rd

Rose at 9 a.m. Breakfast. Curled Lizzie's hair with tongs. Practised on piano. Cleaned after dinner. Went to Chapel at night. Text from *St. John's* Gospel: 'I am the Light of the world &c'. Spoke to Miss Ridgeley after Chapel. Practised tonic at night. Bed at 9.30 p.m.

Monday November 4th 1872

Shied up at 6.30 a.m., at Trafalgar by 7 a.m. Morn fine. Gave Mr.

Walter his book and *Flashes of Light*. Saw Mr. W.B.B., Mrs W.B.B. and Miss Kingscote and C.C.B. examining horse up by upper office at 11 a.m. Saw Ruth and John Mason talking several minutes after dinner. Did not speak to W.B.B. all day. Received nine bags oats, four sharps and two bran in stores. Posted up some this day.

Left Trafalgar at 5.5 p.m. Took home gun stock bought off Tom Jay 1/–. Bought gum 3d., naptha 5d., almanack 6d. Had hinge put in face of watch. Brought two clocks from Greenings and two lamps from Woods for W.B.B. Went straight home. Gave Lizzie 6d. for spelling. Read all evening. Bed at 10 p.m.

Tuesday November 5th 1872

Rose at 5.15, at Trafalgar by 6.10 a.m. Delivered lamps to Mr. Walter. New manager come first thing after breakfast. Came into stores and enquired for Dan Pogson. Went into pit with Pogson. Mr. W.B.B. came into stores and made enquiries about clocks and lamps. Told him the story of them. Chappell going in pit with Taylor of the *Forester* office. Borrow'd my lamp. Hill came into stores and sent his watch to Greenings by me to be repaired. C.C.B. broke the new lamp from Birmingham per Wood, 6/6d. Gave me orders to take it to get it repaired. Did not take it without Mr. W.B.B.'s orders.

Left Trafalgar at 5 p.m., home by 6 p.m. Washing and baking about. Posted two papers, one to Beck and one to Morse. Bought six halfpenny stamps. Cleaned, went to practice at tonic. Bill didn't come. Mr. Waites asked if I couldn't read off a piece. Told him Yes. Enquired how William Green got on. Ask'd me to join the choir on Sunday.

Home at 10 p.m. Mrs. Green treated me with glass of gin before going to bed. Saw Mrs. Cook. She enquired about the wig. I told her I had sold it. Told me she was going to do her hook from old Joe. Said she was owed £35 and over. Bed at 11.10 p.m.

Wednesday November 6th 1872

Shied up at 5.50 a.m., at Trafalgar by 6.15 a.m. Mr. W.B.B. up early, say 7 a.m., and wrote on surveyor's door. Gave me broken lamp to trim and take care of. Took two from stores from Hall and Peddars, Bristol, into the house. Left the two brought from Woods in stores. Smith says W.B.B. caught him asleep last night in weighbox.

Miserable and wet all day. Going to work to night. Posted up all morning. Barling, veterinary surgeon,[101] here before and after dinner. Is in stores. Mason and Jenkins holding serious confab on own affairs in bank. Must make a deposit as soon as possible. Worked for Smith at night. Ennis brought pear pie for me.

Rode home in cart at terrific rate. Home by 1.10 a.m. Bloaters waiting for supper – warm.

Thursday November 7th 1872

Beautiful morn. Shied up at 5.50 a.m., at Trafalgar at 6.30. Second whistle just blown. Pit played both turns. Mr. & Mrs. W.B.B. gone out. Girls alone, did not stay a moment.

Left off at 5 p.m. Two firemen rushed in with cart, old James Brain looking. Collar'd hold and rode down, and joined by blacksmith Tingle. Home at 5.50 p.m. Practised on Concertina. Read paper &c. Bed at 10.30 p.m.

Friday November 8th 1872

Shied up just after whistle blew 6 a.m. At work by 6.30. Pit working first turn, playing second turn. Received stores: paint, dryers, turps, oils, sockets &c. Mr. Walter wish'd me and my stores somewhere else whilst [I was] checking in upper office. C.C.B., Mrs. W.B.B. and Miss Kingscote riding together, was seen by Bilson tip with horses mixed all up. Did not pay in cash this morning. Left posting up stand all day long. Entered up some of stores in ledger. Had Chapel in stores two or three times in day. Mr W.B.B. out on horseback in afternoon. Mr. Davies not seen about Trafalgar all day. Old James Brain came in store for a piece of tar rope. Commenced to write Emily. Did not finish it.

Left work at 5.10 p.m. Home at 6 p.m. Took watch for John Mason, new glass put in, and Hill's to be cleaned.

Practised on concertina with William Green and fiddle. Posted up diary at home. Mrs. Green killed pig this day. Bed at 11 p.m.

Saturday

Shied up at 6 a.m., at work by 6.30 a.m. Two or three waiting for stores. Received offal from E. Little in stores. Pay over by 3 p.m., home by 4 p.m.

Practised piano a little. Tried to get William Green to come to choir on morrow. Failed. Bought one set of shoe brushes 1/– of cheap jack. Paid Mrs. Green bill £2/0/2 for month's board. Paid Long 3d. for paper, Lizzie 1d., boots 16/– from Nobbs.

£2	1	4
	16	
2	17	4

Sunday November 10th 1872

Woke and rose at 8.30 a.m. Morning and all day bitter cold. Did not leave house all day. Went to Chapel at night. Straight home. Practised tonic sol-fa with Amos and Bill for short time. Bed at 10.30 p.m.

Monday November 11th

Shied up at 6.30, up at Trafalgar by 7.10 a.m. Pit worked only one turn. Was told to remind T.B.B. of something next pay [day].

Home at 5.50. Cleaned, went to Abbots Wood with note from T.B.B. to Mr. Edwin Crawshay.[102] Was asked if I knew what the letter was about. Told him I partly knew (I myself copied the letter and its reply). Told him I supposed 'twas concerning the announcement.[103] He said Yes and enquired what the men said about it when they saw it posted. Told him they were scrutinizing it closely, and took reply to Mr. T.B. Brain, Euroclydon.[104]

Found him sitting in shirt sleeves before the fire alone reading paper. Asked me to have something short. Declined. Preferred beer. Sent for servant to draw me some. Told me there was sickness in the house. Mrs. Brain confined and otherwise ill.

Called at Jim Hurcombe's coming back. Had couple glasses beer there. Brought gun stock home to polish. Got home about 10.30. Bill started to work nights at Crump Meadow [Colliery]. Bed directly.

'Went to Abbots Wood with note from T.B.B.' *Abbots Wood House, home of Edwin Crawshay.*

Tuesday November 12th 1872

Kick'd out at 6 a.m., Trafalgar at 6.30. Pit worked one turn. Very cold and frosty. Home at 6 p.m. Did not go to practice at class. Posted up scrap book. Read. Concertina exercise a little. Wrote Beck and Emily and posted them. Bed.

Stamps, paper &c 3d.

Wednesday November 13th

Pit played both turns. At Trafalgar at 6.40 a.m. Very cold. Receiv'd iron in stores, not correct. Saw Mr. Walter in upper office holding confab with Mr. Ridler talking about Alf Goold's generosity and liberality over the dog. Mr. Walter called him a

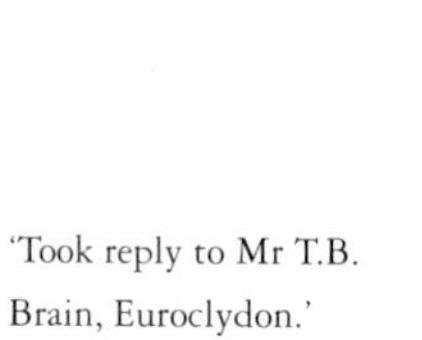

'Took reply to Mr T.B. Brain, Euroclydon.'

shabby coon. Mr. Ridler quite surprised. Received orders from Mr. Walter to order what I wanted from Boud's. Mr. Walter asked me to mend his pipe case. Forgot to take it home.

Left Trafalgar at 5 p.m. Bought 2 pecks of apples[105] for Morse and bespoke two more for Peter Loveridge, and beauties they are. Carried them home. Walked home with Henry Briscoe. Wrote Brogden, Bridgend,[106] about men sent out to New Zealand and enquired if he intends sending any more out. Offered to go if he does. Wrote to Maria Green and told her I am thinking of going out. Promised to send her the letter when I receive it from Messrs. Brogden & Co. Asked if she will come with me if Beck won't. Did not post it. Hesitated about it. Don't think Maria is safe – she will tell her mother about it. Kept the letter from the colonials out of the paper (*Reynolds*). To bed early, 10 o'clock.

Thursday November 14th 1872

Shied up at 5.30 a.m., at Trafalgar at 6.5 a.m. Took fish for Trafalgar. Took parcel for Smith from contractor's office, Lydbrook. Gave it Smith in weighbox. Christie came and enquired for the money he paid me: 3/–. Paid it to Cannock. Borrowed 1/6d. out of petty cash.

Letter from New Zealand. Read it in box. Men seem to be at sixes and sevens at Trafalgar on account of the notices posted.

PORTHCAWL, BRISTOL CHANNEL

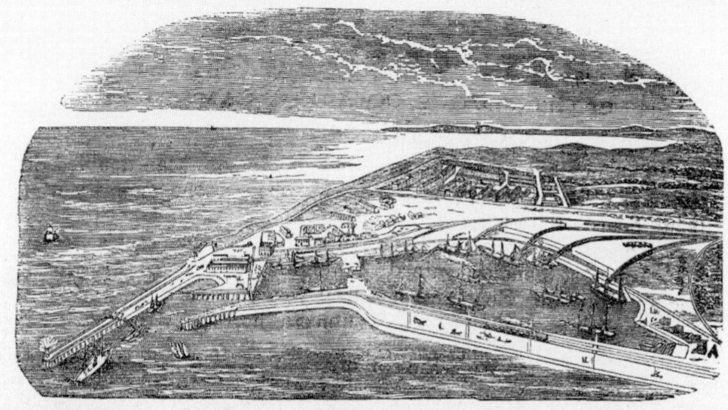

JOHN BROGDEN & SONS,

TONDU

IRON AND COAL WORKS,

BRIDGEND,

Glamorganshire.

SHIPPING PORTS & AGENTS:

Cardiff...EDWARD ROBSON. | **BritonFerry**...JOS. BRIGHT.
Porthcawl. JOHNBROGDEN&SONS | **Swansea**...C. E. STALLYBRASS.

JOHN BROGDEN & SONS are Manufacturers of RAILWAY & MERCHANT IRON, RAILWAY BOLTS and NUTS, RAILWAY PLANT and COAL.

Shippers of Steam, Locomotive Steam, House, Mining, Smiths', and Coking Coal.

The Brand of Iron is J. B. & SONS. The Iron is used largely in Staffordshire, being of a very superior quality.

The Coals and Coke are of the *very purest* description, as proved by analysis, and notoriously the *best* in South Wales for the manufacture of Iron.

Porthcawl is now much enlarged. A Floating Dock and Half-Tide Basin are now completed. There is *no Bar*, and a *clear entrance*, with *deep water*, up to the port. Dues are very moderate. Depth of Water at Neaps, 16 feet; Springs, 27 feet.

117 N.S.W—VIP

'Wrote Brogden, Bridgend, about men sent out to New Zealand.' Slater's Directory, 1868. *Note the nineteenth-century meaning of 'notoriously'.*

Done Mr. Walter's pipe; he is much obliged for it. Did not see W.B.B. all day.

Left work at 5 p.m. Home by 5.30 p.m. Had tea, went to Woods and examined buckets. Couldn't give order – too dear. Ask'd Boud if he could make the galvanized bucket and the price. Says he could make a bucket that would answer our purpose better than the galvanized iron bucket, but it would be cheaper to send for a dozen from wholesale department. Quiet night. Bed at old time, 11 p.m.

Friday Nov. 15th 1872

Shied up at 5.20 a.m., at Trafalgar by 6.10 a.m. Up in office investigating books of C. Meek greater part of day. Money deficient from all directions, receipts never signed, counterfoils vacant &c. Commencing from 1869 with 5d., continuing up to 1872. Should guess about £2,000 to £3,000 short cash. C.C.B. and self investigating tickets.

Bought another half bushel of apples[107] and paid for them, 5/–. Went to Briarley for three quarts of beer. Paid 4d. for one quart. Decent looking girl there. Promised to take can back.

Left Trafalgar at 5.10. Carried fruit home. Briscoe helped me with it. Took it to Morgan, carriers. Paid 8d. for carriage. Wrote Peter Loveridge and Morse. Ordered another bushel of apples from Claytons, Goodrich, Herefordshire. Home to bed at 11 p.m.

6/–

Saturday Nov. 16th 1872

Up at 5.50 a.m., at Trafalgar by 6.10 a.m. Worked in upper office investigating Meek's books. Received one ton bran and two ton half hundredweight of sharps. Had three buckets come from Woods on appro. Mr. Walter holding confab with men about withdrawing the notice [of the 10 per cent wage cut] and extending it a month. Jenkins went home at 1 p.m.

Left work at 3 p.m. Paid Greening for putting glass in watch, 6d. Hill's watch not done. Had two *Foresters, Budget* and *Reynolds* and *Christian World*, 6d. Very cold all the week.

'Had two Foresters.'

At home discovered my writing book left out all day. Every letter pulled about and overhauled. Quite mad with myself. However, couldn't help it. Received letter from Beck, poor lost thing. Wish it had been broke off four years ago. Made gun stock partly and shoeing iron for nailing boots &c on. Panorama of the Franco-Prussian War at the Town Hall. Didn't go. Read a little.

Bed at 10.30 p.m. John not come in. Bill taking supper when I left.

Sunday Nov. 17th 1872

Shied up at 9.30 a.m. Practised tonic sol-fa with Bill all morning. Went upstairs for keys of my box and concertina and, behold, Mrs. Green at my box, reading my letters. Judge my consternation! O that guilty glance. I shall never forget. Downcast eyes, face flushed, red as fire, and messing at my bed &c. Didn't appear to observe me looking at her. Self didn't stop to say a word. Gave her a chance to replace anything that was misplaced. After dinner went up to clean. There was all my things overturned, buttons all over the things, every letter of mine pulled about, not one put back in place. Very sorry to see Mrs. Green commit herself in such a way. Shall say nothing about it, let it drop. Will leave shortly.

Wrote and told Maria. Did not send the letter. William Green and I went to Chapel at night. Very young minister preached from the *Epistle of St. Paul to Timothy* shewing the giver of Godliness in this life and in the one to come. Went home, show'd Greenwood my concertina. House like a public house on a Saturday night. Told Mrs. Green about the letters. She positively denied it. Bed at 11 p.m. Read chapter and prayers.

Monday Nov. 18th 1872

Shied up at 6.30, at Trafalgar by 7.10. Investigating Meek's books all morning. Stores latter part of day. Received very long letter from Maria. Says H.S.L.M.F.T.S.S.M.[108] Did not post up till Thursday. Took letter to Leather Pit[109] and Mosoo's watch to Greenings.

Tuesday Nov. 19th

Late rising. Very cold and wet. Received no letter from Morse but one from Beck. Did not go to investigate books &c. In stores all day.

Left for home at 5 p.m. Went to tonic sol-fa practice. Edwards there. Called for Hill's watch. Not ready. Home at 10. Wrote Maria Green. Bed at 11 p.m.

Wednesday

Rose at 5.30 a.m., at work at 6.30 a.m. Cold in morning, quite moonlight. Received letter from Morse. Mr. Walter in sore fuss about iron. Eleven bars best rivet iron short. Suppose to be cribb'd from the tip. Mr. Walter quite put out. Received leather from Stephens, Monmouth. Two hides, one prepared, one sole leather.

Left Trafalgar at 5 p.m. Fetched Hill's watch from Greening. Tried to get some rivets for soling boots. Bought brad awl, 1d., from Woods. Sold a bucket for Wood, 2/–. Made gun stock at night. Practised with William Green concertina and violin. Bed at 11 p.m.

Thursday Nov. 21st 1872

Rose at 6 a.m., at Trafalgar 6.40 a.m. Lots waiting. Mr. Walter came down to stores and enquired about iron again. Wanted the return of corn from me. Gave it him. Took up fish and Hill's watch. Hill sent 1/– for my trouble. Did not accept it, took 6d., gave the man 6d., dividing it. Received in stores seven bars convex iron, weight 1 ton 1 cwt. 7 lbs. Mr. W.B.B. went out about 3.30 on horseback. Mrs. Brain and Miss Kingscote and family went out with carriage and pair about 4 p.m.

Very busy day. Done no posting up. Home at 5 p.m. Practised concertina and piano. Read paper a little. Bed at 10.30.

Friday Novr. 22nd

Rose at 5.35 a.m., at Trafalgar by 6.10 a.m. Did not see W.B.B. all day. Gave orders for signal wire, pullies second size, sock shovels and vegetable oil. Sold smoothing plane to John Davis, 1/–. It did not work. Smith came to oilhouse and sarcastically remark'd I could if I liked, then went away.

Walk'd home. Mason came down to Bilson by engine. Walk'd to Woodside with him. Called at Bouds, Mason bought lamp and cruett stands for home. Ask'd him to tea. He declined. Wrote Beck to say I was coming Saturday. Sent paper as well. Wrote John Brogden, Bridgend [about emigrating to New Zealand]. Second application. Read paper and practised concertina. Bed 10.40 p.m.

Rivets, stamps and papers 8½d.

Saturday Nov. 23rd 1872

Woke by alarum at 4 a.m. Went back and lay till 5.20 a.m. Woke Bill up. At Trafalgar by 6.10. Fearfully rough and dark and wet, and wind driving violently. Wore two pairs trowsers.

Mr. Walter brought key of upper office and gave it in my charge, and letter from Maria Green. John Mason and Jenkins did not turn up till 9 a.m. Mr. Werner came for key of upper office. Refused to give it to anyone till Mason came. Rained, pouring, most of morning. Thought good deal of going away. Pay commencing between 2 and 3.

Pay day at Trafalgar in the 1870s. Is that C.C. Brain in the centre leaning on the trolley?

Left Trafalgar at 3.45 p.m. Home by 5 p.m. Received wages £2/3/6 from Mr. Walter. Did not pay bill for board and lodge &c. Resolved on going to Gloster about 6.30 p.m. Night very dark. Waited 20 minutes at Newnham. Train 15 minutes late. Arrived at Gloster 10 minutes late, 8.15 instead of 8.5 p.m. Bought head for banjoe and two strings at Mannings.

Up to Wootton by 8.50. Beck look'd jolly. We talked of going out to New Zealand. Did not tell her I thought of going myself. Beck very pleased with my watch and lockett. Bade adieu at 10.40 p.m. Was told P. Loveridge had written me to acknowledge fruit. I said it was not so. Bessie is got well again. Was pressed very hard to stay over Sunday. Excused by saying water would be out[110] and should not be able to get back. All disappointed because I would not stay. Promised to go first fine Sunday and spend the day. Promised to write soon.

Morse and Ben on duty at station. Saw old Uncle Ayres, very pleased to see me. Stood glasses of wine for Morse, Ben, Charlie, Uncle, Arnold and self. Left per mail [train], quite elevated. Walked up from Newnham nearly asleep. Night tempestuous, wind and very dark. Home at 2.50 a.m. All a-bed. Let in by Mr. Green. Bed at 3 a.m.

Sunday Nov. 24th 1872

Shied up at 10.30 a.m. Breakfast, practised on tonic sol-fa &c. Dined on beef and apple pudding. In house all day. Went to Chapel at night. Mr. Waters from Littledean preached beautiful sermon from *St. Paul's Epistle to* [blank]. Words were, 'If ye love not your brother whom ye have seen, how can ye love God whom ye have not seen?' Delightful sermon. A good man and Christian. Spoke of one incident at the commencement of 1872, how he went to a certain place to obtain licence for his dog, and as he went he intended to have mentioned something pertaining to eternal things. But, however, he let it slip and thought he would be seeing him again; but he never saw him again – he was buried a few weeks ago. He told how he regretted not speaking as he intended, how he yielded to the temptation. It was now forever too late. Mr Waters showed most interesting illustrations of the same subject in different views.

After Chapel Amos Hale, Bill and I practised on a few tunes, Mrs. Green looking a little blacker than thunder and quite annoyed. John sat by fire. Came on to rain for the night. Thought to write Morse. Postponed it till Monday, or time convenient.

Monday Novr. 25th

Rose at 6.30 a.m., at work by 7 a.m. Very rough and wet. Made fresh start at phonography, and Mason as well. Worked four hours, hard at it, got through several pages. Determined to learn it. Received letter from Emily at Ogston Hall. Says she is going to outcut me and get married first.

Home at 6 p.m. Work'd hard at phonography. Did not go out anywhere all night. Bill, Jim and Dobbs off at *Globe with Hand*. Was not home till after 11 p.m. Bed at 11.15 p.m. Prayers in the dark. John gone to bed before.

Tuesday Nov. 26th 1872

Shied up at 5.40 a.m., at Trafalgar by 6.30 a.m. Received in stores: naptha lamps (1 dozen), 14 appendage feeders P. valor (1 dozen) from H. Greens, Newport, glass &c. Morning fine but subsequently wet and very rough. Mr. W.B.B. came in stores inspecting the new lamps, trying experiments with them and the burners, and instructing me how to pack and regulate them.

Could not get away till 6 p.m. Took letter for £12/10/– for Curtis of Leather Pit. Did not get the cash. Curtis got the rheumatic, caught cold and laid up. He promised to call on Mr. W.B.B. as soon as able.

Home by 7. Went to watchmakers. Paid £1 for watch. Went to practice, tonic sol-fa. Only six of us there and only four who could sing. William Kitchen had not come at all. Mr. Waites said he wanted to make use of some of us now 'tis getting time we could do something beside doh-ray-me. Received letter or postcard concerning New Zealand from Brogden & Son. Bed at 10.40 p.m. No prayers. More shame.

Wednesday Nov. 27th 1872

Shied up at 6 a.m., at work by 6.40 a.m. Very rough and violent all morning. Received stores in painter's line from Lydney. Practised in morning on phonography. Learned several lessons, work'd hard. Told Mr. Walter the naptha was out. Johnny Mason spoke about getting boxes made. Will cost about 17/– each. Good ones, fit for anything. Did not post up any books at all this day. Took W.B.B.'s tally down first thing this morning that was forgotten yesterday.

Tim Knight came over and learned us a new tune. Dan Pogson came in stores and gave me a pattern of top for leggins cut out &c. Indiarubber, borax and hartshorn dissolved and made a liquid, and past two pieces of cloth together. They will adhere and the same solution will render impervious to wet the leather in boots.

Worked for Smith to night, Ben Bennett check-weighing. Self read some books left in weighbox. Book'd men out. Rode home in cart. Had sausages for supper. Did not go to bed at all. Slept in the chair till 5.20 a.m.

Thursday Novr. 28th 1872

Left home at 5.30 a.m., at Trafalgar by 6.5 a.m. Took fish up. Promised to work on Friday night. Held a little smutty discourse in weighbox with Hodges, Ennis and Smith. Paid Cannock, saddler, 1/10d. for brush. Smith wanted me to work to night. Should have, only no food for the night. Had good dinner.

Matthew Phillips sent a note from his son, W. Phillips from Hereford. Told me there had been a deal turn up on the line. Wants to get a crib [job] here, wants me to speak for him.

Left Trafalgar at 5 p.m. Did nothing after tea. Went to bed at 10 p.m. No prayers again.

Friday Novr. 29th 1872

Shied up at 6.45. Just daylight. John, Bill and Jim got up same time. Terrible scuffle for boots &c. Rode up part of way with C. Cotton. The Brain brothers up at 7.20 a.m. I was ashamed to open door. Pogson remarked that I was late. Churchill said old

'Held a little smutty discourse in weighbox.'

Jimmy had been enquiring about me and wants to see me. Promised to go some day and see them.

Mr. Walter enquiring about springs from the Lileshall Company,[111] quite in a concern about them. Cannot bring our account to bear with Lileshall's invoice of £121 odd. Received 20 bags oats in store from E. Little. Put sacks in bags to go to Robinson for more oats. Little's man says he left one sack of sharps last time more than quantity.

Worked after 5 p.m. for Smith. Wet first part of the night.

Cinderford Ironworks towards the end of the nineteenth century. John, Bill and Jim Green worked here.

Lent two sacks to workmen. Put them in weighbox. Dry at midnight. Book'd out men at midnight. Home at 1.40 a.m. Did not go to bed. Slept by fire.

Saty morning Novr. 30th and last

Up at Trafalgar at 6.10 a.m. Men booked in by 6 a.m. Rope from Newall's took for deep pit. Smith put bags out in the dirt and pouring rain to get wet. Began to reprimand him for it. Said he would do it again. Put bags inside the door and while I sent note down pit Smith kick'd them outside. I collar'd Smith by nobs and scruffed him a bit. Gave him a challenge. Not accepted. Went down to weighbox again. Smith said he would like to give me a bloody good hiding. Gave him a fair offer. Smith told some he would accommodate me going home. Self quite open for the attack.

Home by 4 p.m. Couldn't resolve on going to Gloucester.

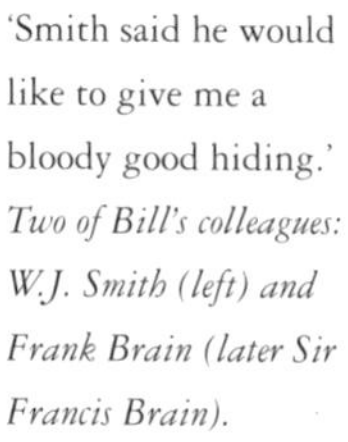

'Smith said he would like to give me a bloody good hiding.' *Two of Bill's colleagues: W.J. Smith (left) and Frank Brain (later Sir Francis Brain).*

Wrote Brogden & Sons, London, a postcard. Wrote Morse and Beck. Sent a paper each. Promised to go next Sunday if fine.

Bought two flannel shirts and two pairs socks, writing paper &c 9d. Home and considered whether to go or not to Gloster. Read papers &c. Bed at 10 p.m.

Total spent 12/9d.

Sunday Dec 1st 1872

Rose at 9.40. Did not go to Chapel in morning. Practised tonic sol-fa with Bill. Wrote a hymn out *Sing a Hymn to Jesus* for Amos Hale. Went to Chapel at night. Mr. Preece preached Mrs. Chiver's funeral sermon. Very good. Announced Mr. Bloomfield of Gloster would preach there next Sunday. Home direct from Chapel. Bed at 10 p.m. John not come home.

Monday Decr. 2nd 1872

Rose at 7 a.m., at Trafalgar by 7.20 a.m. Lots waiting for me. Went to weighbox, enquired if Smith work'd or not. Said I could work if I had got a mind. Told him I would work and did not say any more then. Ben Bennett remarked it was a beautiful day. Left weighbox and put Cotton's oil. Cotton sent it back and said I was to measure it. Refused. Cotton brought it back. Did not put any more, took a pint out, Cotton had to go with that.

Done no posting up. Sent for corn. Had Mosooo's watch to take to Benjamin Greenings to regulate, and 4d. to pay him. Had orders to take clock to be repaired. Fresh orders, to see W.B.B. before taking it. Sent a message to tell W.B.B. the reason I did not call. Had a bit of chat with Jane. Got very close against her. Told her how I should like to.

Walked home alone and home by 1.40 a.m. Spent 8d. Lent 4d. to Jarrett.

Tuesday Decr. 3rd

Beautiful day. Shied up at 5.30 a.m., at Trafalgar by 6.15 a.m. W.B.B. about early, looking for me whilst I went to shit. Received oil from Read & Jackson, Bristol. Casks leaking badly. 214 gallons, 2/9th by measure. Told of naptha being at Nelson Road.

Went to see about clocks &c from Greenings. Mr. Werner sent his watch by me to be regulated. Did not take it. Forgot. Greening promised to put it all right in a twink when I take it there. Forgot also Ben Bennett's letter.

Saw Bessy Tingle going home. Told her I was going to take her for a walk after school. Home at 5.40. Fetched clock from Greenings and returned directly. Practised on concertina and violin. Went to class at 8 p.m., done at 9.50. Took Bessie Tingle home. Nicely done, an amiable catch. Home at 10 p.m. Bed at 11 p.m.

Wednesday Dec. 4th 1872

Beautiful morn. Uncurled at 5.45. At work at 6.30 a.m. Mr.

Werner enquired about his watch. Told him Greening would put it right for him in a few days. Gave him change out of a 1/– for something Benjamin Greening had done. Brought W.B.B.'s alarum. W.B.B. off on Arabian [horse] at 10.30 a.m. Coachman behind. Thinking about Ellen Preece. Intend writing again. 'Tis bad to be unfriendly.

Worked for Smith in evening. Brought in candles. Weigh'd them, 1 cwt. 2 quarters 10 lbs. Booked men out. Copied out check list [shorthand illegible]

Left pit about 1.10. Rode home in cart. Sharply freezing. Ground very hard. Letter from J. Brogden & Sons.

Thursday Decr. 5th 1872

Beautiful morning. Very sharp frost. Took fish up in morning. Had Brogden's letter to read. Jenkins cut my hair. Jane sent some soup. Received last of oats, 200 bushels, and four sacks sharps in stores and glazier sprigs.[112] Ben Bennett and F. was thinking of taking up a bit of money for horse and cart and start coal hauling for the colliers at Trafalgar colliery.

Mr. John Griffiths related anecdote relative to Votaire's[113] attendant on his death bed. Saw Cooper for first time at weigh machine at Strip[-and-at-it-Pit]. Came on to rain later in day.

Home at 6 p.m. Wrote shorthand a little. Played a rare old school game with Lizzie. Bed at 10.30 p.m.

Friday Decr. 6th 1872

Shied up at 5.50, at Trafalgar by 6.30 a.m. Received letter from Emily requesting me to pay her washing account. Says she is in trouble about it. Wrote her a line to console her.

Paid in petty cash, 8/10½d. Read *Forrester*. Addressed it and sent to Beck. Made a bootjack. Aaron Walkley made me eight corners for a new box. Tapped two oil casks last thing. Mrs. W.B.B., Miss Kingscote and coachman went out for equestrian exercise at 5 p.m.

Left Trafalgar at 5.10 p.m. Whitston and Read dividing the new 1000 yard rope for dipple all evening. Rode down with Tom

Jayne. Bought a 3d. stamp for young Jayne and six halfpenny ones for papers &c. Bought 6d. bottle of coaguline for cementing. Paid for umbrella and No. 1 cyphering book 4d. Practised concertina one hour. Mrs. Green killed pig. Bed at 10.40 p.m.

Total spent 3/10d.

Saturday Decr. 7th 1872

Pay day. Beautiful morning, not cold. Shied up at 5.30 a.m., at Trafalgar by 6 a.m. Harris brought watch to be raffled for. Draw'd up form for him, paid Aaron Walkley 3d. for corner irons for box. Thinking about going to Gloster this evening. Reminded Mr. Tom [T.B. Brain] of what he desired me to. Gave me 2/6d. for going to Abbotts Wood on November 11th. Mr. W.B.B. told me he had been in stores but had not taken anything. I told him what went on Saturday previous [when had row with Smith over bags put out in rain]. Smith did not pay me for working for him. Did not see him.

Engine staff at Trafalgar Colliery, 1883

Left Trafalgar at 4 p.m. Bought *Budget* and *Reynolds*. Had strong intention of going to Gloster. Postponed it. Weather looked very threatening for tempest. Got home at 4.50, read paper &c, shorthand a little, but no quiet to do anything at my lodge. Bought hair oil 3d., Lizzie 1d., Polly 2½d., Mrs. Green £2/0/5 for month's board. Bed at 10.50 p.m. or 11 p.m.

Spent £2/1/2

Sunday Decr. 8th 1872

Rolled out at 9.30. Breakfast not ready till 10 a.m. Too late for Chapel. Quite undecided about starting for Gloucester. Not sure how the trains run, and weather very uncertain. Remained till after dinner uncleaned and ill tempered. Brushed up after dinner. Tonic sol-fa'd a bit. Took tea with Mrs. Green and F. Cooksey. Chapel in evening. Heard Mr. Bloomfield of Gloster. Very interesting sermon out of *Acts of Apostles*. Words were, 'And when they were loosed they returned to their own Company.' Beautiful illustrations all throughout sermon. Many very amusing anecdotes in discourse. Left Chapel, went straight home. Talked &c, an hour or so, and bed at 10 p.m.

Monday Decr 9th 1872

Shied up at 6.30, at Trafalgar at 6.40 a.m. Fine morn, but most rough and windy all Sunday night. Never heard it so rough before. Lots of places partly stripped from wind. Mr. W.B.B. went off early in morning. Observed light in window as I passed by front. Smith sent 6/8d., my coin for two nights' work, and ask'd for glue for papers, which I sent him. Also informed him that I would work Tuesdays and Thursdays instead of as heretofore. Not much posted, [only] Mosooo's order to Mr. Davis for 12/–. Mr. Walter sent down details for me to copy out. Work'd all spare time at them. Finished them by 5.30 p.m. Told Mr. Walter how I had been situated, and took my respectable hook.

Rode home with F.G. Brothers. Home before 6 p.m. Wrote good advice to Emily [Cook of Cheltenham]. Too late for post.

Got playing with Lizzie, and she knock'd down the ink. Mrs. Green and I had a row for damaging her property. Went to chemist, got two pennyworth of salts of lemon and got a lot of it out. Did not speak afterwards all the evening to her. Thought about leaving there. Bed about 10.20 p.m.

Spent 2d.

Tuesday Decr. 10th 1872

Shied up at 5.30 a.m., at Trafalgar at 6.15 a.m. Received box of [metal] files from Osbald Diston. Checked them with John Mason. Packet of assorted ward files not to hand. Busy all day and all behind into the bargain. Posted letter to Emily in evening.

Work'd for Smith this evening. Ben Bennett and Tim Knight and self practised tonic sol-fa.

Left work at 12.50 midnight. Posted letter for James Brain and one for Ben Bennett. Walked home with poor old Apperley. Old man obliged to lie down frequently on account of something in his thigh.

Home at 1.30 a.m. No letter from Beck or Morse. Only a fortnight since I heard or seen anything of them. Must go up Saturday week. Bones left for my supper. Something like pie, couldn't tell what it was. Bed at 2 a.m.

1d. spent.

Wednesday Decr. 11th 1872

Shied up at 5.50 a.m., Trafalgar by 6.30 a.m. John Mason not here all day. R. Jay telling John Hale that his son sends his love and makes enquiries how he is getting on, and tells him that he earned £15 for November month, and says that this month he will be earning over £20/–/– himself for December.

Mr. Walter wants statistic of corn offal &c for October, November and December. Complains of E. Little's bill being twice as long as it was in September month. C.C.B. and self working it out. Mr. Walter came to me as he went to dinner and told me he had found out the secret.[114] Felt quite pleased about it.

Self went to stable when a letter was given me from Cheltenham from poor Era Holland who wants me to write at once. Wants some consideration upon it.

Went to class at 7 p.m. Mr. Waites and I had a little confab together upon singing and told me he had a bill for us to discharge, adding that the way to discharge it was by giving strict attention to singing every spare hour we had. Promised him we would. Left class at 8 p.m.

Called on Mrs. Cook.[115] Spent an hour there. Told her about letter from Era Holland. Planned a note but was advised not to write to Holland. Walked previous to that down town with Charles Ashley. Told me he had sent off cheque for £10 for harmonium to London. Home about 9.30. Practised in *Golden Chain* half hour. Bed at 11.30.

Thursday Decr. 12th 1872

Rolled out at 5.30 a.m., at Trafalgar at 6.10 a.m. Beautiful morn. Hard frost. Took up fish. Cat got one sole out of pail. Cleaned up stores. Took old shovels to old iron stack. Others for repair. Labelled oil and ordered stores. Wrote Beck. Too late for post.

Ask'd Smith if it would be any advantage for me to work on Friday night instead of Thursday as I arranged. Was told 'No'. Accordingly took my own turn. Went to house to beg tea. John Mason sent lad for cider. Came back with bottle full. Each one sent a verse to Jane, the first verse an introduction to the second, which was a comedy, and the third thanks for kindness.

Beautiful and fine at midnight. Cold. Home at 1.30 a.m. Bed at 2 a.m.

Friday Decr. 13th 1872

Rolled up at 6.10 a.m., at Trafalgar by 7 a.m. Men waiting, some gone without their things. Dan Pogson came in stores and told me I stayed too long in sheets. Acknowledged I had lain too long.

Pogson said he had been talking to Chapel about his keeping the key [on] nights when I happened to work. Shan't be sorry when night work's done. Woman brought besoms, four dozen

'Rolled out at 5.40a.m., at Trafalgar by 6a.m. Beautiful morn.'

and eight. Told me it was six dozen. Counted them and paid for accordingly. 16 short. Woman quite annoyed at my counting them. Told me none of other bailiffs or storekeepers ever did.

Finished up the new tool book. Jane wanted me to come and take her to Lydbrook to see dissolving views. Arranged with Mason to accompany her. Jane sent cider over, sweetened and all right.

Bought *Forrester*. Wrote at home in pencil *Lazy Dick* history.

Bed at 10.15. Wished no one good night. Bought cyphering book 4d., comb 6d., pins 1d., pipe tube 1d., stamp 2d., *Forester* 2d. and something else 3d.

Total 1/7d. spent.

Saturday Decr. 14th 1872

Rolled out at 5.40 a.m., at Trafalgar by 6 a.m. Beautiful morn. Came on wet. Smith left early to go to Gloster. Self resolved on going in afternoon. Received letter from Emily, very kind one. Borrowed 8/– from petty cash.

Left Trafalgar at 3 p.m. Bought *Reynolds* and *Budget* 2d. Home by 4 p.m. Raining steadily. Cleaned up and went to Gloucester. Waited Newnham about an hour and ten minutes. 5.50 train two hours late. Saw John Lewis. Had two glasses of ale with him, 6d. Bought two hairpins for Beck 1/6d., lead 2d., Christmas card 6d. Took Beck the bit of spar {crystalline mineral} I and Jim Brain cut out of the old Rockey and Starkey cut-out[116] in August 1872.

'5.50 train two hours late.' *Newnham station.*

Beck very cool. Would not kiss or be kissed. Arranged for Sunday. Stayed till 10.30.

Took Morse's carpet bag back. Came back by Mrs. Lea's. Pitched tent for the night on sofa. Beck and I invited to Christmas party at Mrs. Lea's.

Spent 4/9d.

Sunday Decr. 15th 1872

Wet morning. Rolled off sofa at 9.20 a.m., unrefreshed enough. Took cup of tea and bit of breakfast at Mrs. Lea's. Learned a tune off Miss Price. Mrs. Lea shewed me her piano and I rattled it a bit. Left there just after church were out. Arrived just in time for dinner at Morse's. Partook of boiled swine, no pudding. Didn't have much chatter. Rowland Morse and I sung a little. Rowland had bad cold. Saw his intended come in.

Left for Wootton Hill Cottage at 3.40. Rowland came along to the crossing. Beck just ready when I arrived there. Went to Uncle Cross's to tea. Robertses and Longs all there. E. Roberts and Jeffries came in. Had no confab. Partook of very social, comfortable tea. Mrs. Roberts spoke very little. Dolly, dear little thing, singing most of time. Quite agreeable with me. Mrs. Roberts put the spoons in my pocket.[117] Peter ludicrously amusing, dry, Robert assisting him. Made very welcome there. Will remember it long. Left at 8.35 p.m.

Beck and I called at Morse's going home. Beck vexed at my sneering. Felt very sorry but didn't show anything. Got home about 9.30 p.m. at Wootton. Mary provided beautiful beef pie for supper. Poor Mary has been ill with ague. Spoke most kind and respectful of Beck attending to her when unwell.

Sat till after 10 p.m. Then went out. Beck would come without anything on to prevent cold. Wouldn't let her come out. Bade good night. Hid in the shrubs. Beck came out and look'd round, went back and lock'd up, not seeing me. Rung the bell then, talked a little. Squeezed Beck very tight below the belt, she didn't mind it much. Arranged about getting married in April next. Time is short. I must make a strenuous effort. Poor Beck.

What a shame keeping her and self homeless so long. Left her when clock struck 11 p.m.

Met Morse just down the road coming to meet me. Told him we had arranged for winding up in April next. Morse pleased to hear it. Slept in grease house [at Gloucester station] an hour and a half. Beautiful night. Had company up from Newnham to Littledeane. Home at 2.30 a.m.

Monday Decr. 16th 1872

Morning fine, but wet greater part of day. Shied up about 6.30 a.m., at Trafalgar by 6.50 a.m. Most of men in pit. Mr. Walter want'd to know what I wanted in stores. Left order for naptha, vegetable oil &c in upper office.

Left Trafalgar about 5 to 5 p.m. Got home by 5.45 p.m. and called at Greenings for Ben Bennett's watch and order for cake at Tyndalls. Watch not found, not done. Home, quite wet. Changed clothes. Wrote some of *The History of Lazy Dick* out. Finished the chapter. Read *Reynolds*, cut out selections &c. Bed at 10 p.m.

Tuesday Decr. 17th 1872

Night work tonight. At Trafalgar by 6 a.m. when whistle blew. Wet nearly all day, very unpleasant. Mr. Werner, Dan Pogson, Frank Brain and self practising tonic sol-fa. Wrote out the piece *Stand on the Rock* in tonic sol-fa for class [to be] started at Ruardean this day. Mr. T.B. Brain come from W.B.B. at London. Been off a week. John Mason been away at Cinderford most of the day. C.C.B.'s brother from Connells, Cheltenham, here, soliciting orders. Mr. Walter up here in stores enquiring about the filter from Lipscombe, London. Wrote shorthand a good bit this day. Commenced writing to Beckie. Left my food for Smith whom I got to work.

Left Trafalgar at 5.30 p.m. Mr Walter wanted me to go to Cinderford to take back Mr. Hodge's concert tickets. Met the man that brought them and delivered them to him. Bought 3d. of linseed oil from Cordwins.

Whilst out Mrs. Cook called to see me. Met her coming home. Told me she had been. I was quite sharp with her. Wanted some money. Told her I would meet her by the barn. Most awfully cold. Took her into barn and rammed her backwards. Gave her 3/4d. Told me she would hook it this week. Wanted me to forge a character for her.

Got home about 9.20. Polished Jim Hurcombe's gun stock and four sticks. Bed at 11.30 p.m.

Linseed oil 3d.

Wednesday Decr. 18th 1872

Beautiful day. Up at 5.30, at work by 6.10 a.m. Very cold wind. Brought two sticks for T. Surby. Mr. Walter enquiring what was the result of the tickets and concert last night. Emptied oil casks, vegetable and olive, and waste bag. Mr. W.B.B. not come home. Been off nine days. Mr. Werner and Dan and I practised tune on tonic sol-fa. Lent Mosooo *Bristol Tune Book* all day and didn't get it back same day.

Worked for wages at night. Read good deal of *Uncle Tom's Cabin*, the chapter of Evangeline and Augustine St. Clare's death and the auction. Was struck most impressively with some of its beautiful contrasts and the extensive range of mind of the writer.

Left Trafalgar at 12.20 a.m. Home at 1.15 a.m. Fire in. Supper in corner. Fish come and laying under the table. Felt hungry for a fish. Took one out of basket and partly toasted it and ate it for supper. Bed at 2 a.m.

Thursday Decr. 19th 1872

Wet and dull morning. Shied up at 5.40 a.m., at Trafalgar by 6.20 a.m. Brought up fish for house, sent it in by Henry Jones. Thinking about poor Uncle Tom a good deal that I read the night before. Did not see Mr. W.B.B. Not come home, I suppose.

Home at 5.30. Wrote Beck a long letter. Didn't keep a copy of it. Spoke about Polly and company on Sunday. Promised Beck a respirator to prevent her [illegible] me so much. Promised to marry her when the days grow long again. No more flinching and shirking. Receiv'd Gloster paper from Beck. Went to bed at 10.30 p.m.

Gloucester  Journal.

GENERAL ADVERTISER FOR CITY AND COUNTY, AND NEIGHBOURING SHIRES.

VOL. CLI.——No. 7836.] {Established by ROBERT RAIKES, 1722.} SATURDAY, DECEMBER 14, 1872. {Registered for Transmission Abroad.} PRICE, THREEPENCE. Stamped, Threepence-Halfpenny.

ELECTION OF VERDERER.

To the Freeholders of the County of Gloucester.

MY LORDS AND GENTLEMEN,—

SINCE writing my letter dated the 7th inst., and which appeared in the Gloucester papers of last Saturday, I have had an opportunity of perusing the report contained in the *Gloucester Journal* of the 11th of July, 1863, of the Election of Verderers which took place on the previous Monday, and the result is, that I am more than ever convinced that every right thinking and impartial person will agree with me that Sir Thomas H. C. Boevey is, in every sense of the word, honourably bound by the arrangement entered into on the 1st July, 1863, between the other gentlemen, who were then Candidates, and myself. Whilst I admit that the memorandum is correctly quoted as to the words, by Sir Thomas, in his address of the 6th inst., it is to be observed that the word "themselves" appearing in such quotation was not written in italics in the original. The italics are Sir Thomas's own, and, therefore, no such stress is to be laid upon the word as Sir Thomas would seem to wish there should be. Who, knowing the circumstances, can for a moment doubt that Sir Thomas was privy to the arrangement which he now seeks to ignore. He was not an outsider merely, like any other Elector, but was the personal friend of two or three of the Candidates, actively interfered, as I believe, in promoting their Election against me; was present at the Election itself, and proposed Mr. Charles Bathurst, one of the signitaries of the memorandum containing the arrangement above referred to, after several previous speakers had congratulated one another, and the County, that the threatened contest had been averted by the retirement of Mr. Onslow and myself. Let these facts, and the circumstance that the memorandum was signed very late on the Wednesday before the Election, be borne in mind, and I shall have no doubt as to what your opinion upon the issue raised between Sir Thomas H. C. Boevey and myself will be.

But even assuming that Sir Thomas was neither party nor privy to the arrangement, I allege that beyond all doubt the spirit of it was, that neither the then Candidates nor their friends should, directly or indirectly, oppose me at the next vacancy; and I feel sure that this view of the transaction will be adopted by others who took part in the negotiations, and were parties to the memorandum.

I have the honor to be,
My Lords and Gentlemen,
Your obedient servant,
ALFRED GOOLD.

Newnham, 13th Nov., 1872. 6253

To the Freeholders of the County of Gloucester.

MY LORDS AND GENTLEMEN,—

A VACANCY in the Office of Verderer of Her Majesty's Forest of Dean having occurred by the death of my late friend, Mr. Edward Owen Jones, I beg to offer myself as a Candidate, and respectfully solicit your support.

My late Father and Grandfather were honoured by being elected Verderers of our Forest, and, should you do me the honour to elect me to fill the present vacancy, you may rely on my earnest endeavours to perform the duties with strict impartiality.

I observe in the Gloucester Papers of last Saturday an address by Mr. Alfred Goold, who also offers himself as a Candidate for the present vacancy, in which address Mr. Goold appears to present to you his claim to be elected upon the ground that in the year 1862 (meaning, I conceive, 1863) when the last election took place, and when he was a candidate, he retired...

Gloucester Union.

PERSONS willing to Contract with the Guardians of the above Union for the supply of the undermentioned Articles, are requested to send sealed TENDERS, addressed to me, with Samples, to the Union Workhouse, on or before the hour of TWELVE o'clock at noon, on Monday the 23rd day of December instant, viz.:—FLOUR, MEAT, CHEESE, BACON, GROCERIES, including TEA, at the fixed price of 2*s.* per lb., MALT, *Good* FRESH BUTTER, *Good* SALT Ditto, COAL, DRAPERY, and LEATHER.

The Contract to commence on Monday, the 30th day of December, 1872, and to expire on Saturday, the 29th day of March, 1873.

The Guardians do not pledge themselves to accept the lowest or any Tender.

Forms of Tender and other particulars can be obtained on application to the Master of the Workhouse at his Office here.

By order of the Board of Guardians,
L. G. HUBERT MAYER, Clerk.

Poor Law Offices, Gloucester Workhouse,
12th December, 1872. 6464

GLOUCESTER AND BERKELEY CANAL.

TENDERS FOR MATERIALS.

THE Directors will be prepared to receive on Wednesday, the 1st day of January, TENDERS for the SUPPLY of such MATERIALS as may be required by the Company in the year 1873.

All Tenders must be sent in not later than Ten o'clock on the morning of that day, and be marked "Tender" on the outside. HENRY WADDY, Secretary.

Canal Office, Gloucester, 14th Dec., 1872. 6520

SECURITIES WANTED. — £6,000, £4,000, £2,000, and several Sums of £1,000 each are ready to be advanced on good landed securities.—Apply to Messrs. G. and F. R. Moore, Solicitors, 2, Church Street, Warwick. 6503

CHRISTMAS, 1872.

J. WILLIAMS'S

GAME AND POULTRY SHOW,

On THURSDAY next, Dec. 19, 1872;—Upwards of

2000 Head to Choose From.—No Foreign.

Northgate Street, Gloucester, Dec. 12th. 6484

GLOUCESTER INFIRMARY.

PERSONS willing to Contract for the Supply of the undermentioned ARTICLES, to be delivered at the Gloucester Infirmary during the ensuing Quarter, to commence on the 1st day of January next, and to terminate on the 31st day of March next, are requested to send Tenders to the Secretary (properly sealed), before twelve o'clock, on Thursday, the 19th day of December instant.

Household Bread, in Loaves of 2lbs. 8oz. each, at per Loaf, the Bread to be baked twelve hours before delivery.

Butchers' Meat, of best quality, at per score; average quantity per week 380lbs. more or less, if required, to be supplied in the following proportions:—

Beds of Beef	80 lbs.
Rear ends	60 "
Sides of Mutton—divided into joints ...	240 "
	380

Such portions of fat of the Mutton to be cut off as may be required.

Good Purple Potatoes at per Sack.	*Black Tea, per chest of 1 cwt.
Fresh Butter, per lb.	*Coffee, per lb.
*Cheese, per cwt.	*Cocoa, per lb.
*Ale, per gallon.	*Moist Sugar, per lb.
*Flour (best seconds), per bushel.	*Rice, per cwt.
*Candles, per dozen lbs.	Coal, per ton.
	*Soap, best Yellow, per cwt.
	*Scotch Oatmeal, per cwt.

Tenders for all the Articles marked * must be accompanied by Samples.

By order of the Weekly Board,
T. H. PIKE, Secretary.

December 12th, 1872. 6486

CHRISTMAS PRESENTS AND NEW YEAR'S GIFTS.

A. MANSELL

Respectfully invites attention to her large and varied assortment of

Christmas Cards, Photographs, Photographic Scrap Albums, Almanacks, Pocket Books, Diaries, &c., &c.

Any popular work may be had to read, either by subscribers or non-subscribers from

MANSELL'S CIRCULATING LIBRARY, 7, COLLEGE COURT, GLOUCESTER.

A SUITABLE PRESENT FOR CHRISTMAS.

THE PHOTOGRAPHS (BY BILLING) OF THE

NEW REREDOS IN GLOUCESTER CATHEDRAL,

(The gift of the Freemasons of the Province),

PUBLISHED IN THREE SIZES,

By A. MANSELL, 7, College Court, Gloucester.

WINTER FASHIONS.

DEBENHAM & FREEBODY are now making their principal SHOW of FASHIONS for the Winter Season. The Collection of Novelties is very large, and includes every approved Home and Foreign production, as well as their own Special Styles. Attention is especially invited to the COSTUME, MANTLE, MILLINERY, SILK, LACE, BALL DRESS, and OUTFITTING SHOW ROOMS.

A Separate Department is organised for the execution of orders by post.

The Winter number of their "New Fashion Book" is now ready, and will be forwarded by post on receipt of six stamps.

CAVENDISH HOUSE, CHELTENHAM.

BASS AND CO.'S
EAST INDIA PALE, AND FAMILY ALES,
BURTON-ON-TRENT.

October Brewings now in full perfection, of their Agent,

EDWARD EAST,

IMPORTER OF WINES AND SPIRITS,

18, Southgate Street, and 85, Northgate Street, Gloucester.

Silk, Shawl, & Mantle Warehouse, & Household and Family Linen Depot.

12 AND 13, NORTHGATE STREET, GLOUCESTER.

THOMAS DENTON

Begs respectfully to announce that he is now making a

SPECIAL SHOW of NOVELTIES for the AUTUMN and WINTER SEASONS.

HE has made his entire Stock replete and most unusually full, having himself, and the Managers in the leading Departments, just returned from the Markets, which have been visited for the purpose of selecting FASHIONS of the NEWEST and MOST APPROVED DESIGN.

The following Branches contain large and varied assortments:—

THE DRESSES are unusually well-furnished, and contain the new season textures in French and English Dress Fabrics, Plain and Striped Velveteens, Costumes, Polonaises, &c., &c.

THE MANTLES AND MILLINERY comprise the latest productions, the former containing a large and handsome Stock of Real Seal and Real Seal-trimmed Beaver Jackets.

He would also mention the following Departments. The space will not allow of particular enumeration:—

LADIES' UNDERCLOTHING AND CHILDREN'S DEPARTMENT.

Shawls, Lace, and Fancy Goods, Gloves, Ribbons, Hosiery, and a very large Stock of Flannels Blankets, and Household and Family Linens.

HE RESPECTFULLY SOLICITS AN INSPECTION OF HIS STOCK.

WAREING AND SON,

3, WESTGATE STREET, GLOUCESTER,

SHIRT TAILORS,

LONGCLOTH, LINEN FRONTS, AND FITTINGS.

A Quality	6s. 6d. each	Six for 36s.
B Quality	7s. 6d. each	Six for 42s.
C Quality	[illegible]	Six for 48s.

FOREIGN AND COLONIAL GOVERNMENT TRUST.

(FIFTH ISSUE.)

BEARING 5 PER CENT. INTEREST.

To be issued at £88.

Thus paying about £5 13*s.* 6*d.* per cent.

Trustees.

The Right Hon. Lord Westbury.
Lord Eustace Cecil, M.P.
George Wodehouse Currie, Esq.
G. M. W. Sandford, Esq.
Philip Rose, Esq.

WITHIN less than a year from the fourth issue of this Trust, the Trustees have been induced, at the solicitation of many of the holders in the former trusts, again to offer to the public an opportunity for investing in this now well-known security.

The nominal amount of the present issue will not be less than £500,000, or more than £1,000,000; but the Trustees do not pledge themselves to invest the whole amount that may be subscribed.

Though forming a distinct and separate Trust this will be similar in character to the last issue. The Trustees and Management will be the same. The securities to be selected and purchased by the Trustees will be of a similar class, viz., Stocks or obligations of Foreign or Colonial Governments, States, Sovereigns, or Municipalities, or the shares and obligations of any Foreign-Railway or other undertaking which has a guarantee of, or is subsidized by, a Foreign or Provincial Government or Municipal Authority; and no more than one-tenth of the amount subscribed will be invested in any one stock or security.

The responsibility of the Trustees in connection with the purchase of the securities is limited to making the selection to the best of their judgment. The amount of each security purchased will be specified in the schedule to the Trust Deed, which will be signed by the Trustees as soon as the securities are delivered.

The present issue will be made at the price of £88 for a £5 per cent. certificate, yielding the investor about £5 13*s.* 6*d.* per cent. per annum free of Income Tax, with the additional advantage of the drawings and reversion.

The results of the former issues are as follows:—

The £6 per cents. of 1868, issued at £85, are now quoted at £108, or a premium of £23 per cent.

The £5 per cents. of 1870, issued at £80, are now quoted at £98, or a premium of £18 per cent.

The £6 per cents. of 1871, issued at £92, are now quoted at £102, or a premium of £10 per cent.

The £6 per cents. of 1872, issued at £95, are now quoted at £104, or a premium of £9 per cent.

For each £88 of the total amount subscribed will be issued a Certificate of £100, with interest-coupons attached, bearing £5 per cent. interest, payable at the banking-house of Messrs. Glyn, Mills, Currie, and Co., half-yearly, on the 15th of June and the 15th of December; the first coupon for about five months' interest falling due on the 15th day of June next.

The annual receipts by the Trustees will be first applied, after deducting the limited amount of expenses, in paying the interest upon the Certificates. The excess will be applied as a sinking fund in repaying the Certificates at *par* by annual drawings, to be made in the presence of a notary public.

The Trust will last for twenty-five years, at the expiration of which time it is estimated that a large proportion of the Certificates will, in all probability, have been paid off, and that a considerable amount of securities will still remain for distribution as a reversion. The Trust will, therefore...

'Receiv'd Gloster paper from Beck.'

174 UNCLE TOM'S CABIN.

place where Haley's gang of men and women sat in their chains. She would glide in among them, and look at them with an air of perplexed and sorrowful earnestness; and sometimes she would lift their chains with her slender hands, and then sigh wofully as she glided away. Several times she appeared suddenly among them with her hands full of candy, nuts, and oranges, which she would distribute joyfully to them, and then be gone again.

Tom watched the little lady a great deal before he ventured on any overtures towards acquaintanceship. He knew an abundance of simple acts to propitiate and invite the approaches of the little people, and he resolved to play his part right skilfully. He could cut cunning little baskets out of cherry-stones, could make grotesque faces on hickory-nuts, or odd-jumping figures out of elder pith, and he was a very Pan in the manufacture of whistles of all sizes and sorts. His pockets were full of miscellaneous articles of attraction, which he had hoarded in days of old for his master's children, and which he now produced, with commendable prudence and economy, one by one, as overtures for acquaintance and friendship.

The little one was shy, for all her busy interest in everything going on, and it was not easy to tame her. For a while she would perch like a canary bird on some box or package near Tom while busy in the little arts aforenamed, and take from him, with a kind of grave bashfulness, the little articles he offered. But at last they got on quite confidential terms.

"What's little missy's name?" said Tom at last, when he thought matters were ripe to push such an inquiry.

"Evangeline St. Clare," said the little one, "though papa and everybody else call me Eva. Now, what's your name?"

"My name's Tom; the little chil'en used to call me Uncle Tom 'way back thar in Kentuck."

"Then I mean to call you Uncle Tom, because, you see, I like you," said Eva. "So, Uncle Tom, where are you going?"

"My name's Tom" (page 174).

'Read good deal of *Uncle Tom's Cabin.*'

Friday Decr. 20th 1872

Shied up at 5.20, at Trafalgar at 6.10 a.m. Precious wet, miserable morning. Got damp going to work. Wet greater part of day. C.C.B. came in stores and told me I had got the best job after all. He tried to look my work up. Self didn't satisfy him upon anything, nor did I intend to. Mr. Werner, Dan Pogson, Frank Brain and self practising tonic sol-fa dinner time. *Foresters* 3d., one to Beck.

Mr. W.B.B. returned from London. Mr. Walter called for five or six of us to go and assist and carry luggage. Got there just after it was all carried in. Mr. Walter said we were all too late. Did not speak to W.B.B. at all. All up at Trafalgar House. Mr. W.B.B. exhibiting his new wonders from London. Girls all stopping up to see them.

Work'd for Smith at night. Smith got almost familiar again. Ennis didn't come all night. Jarrett and I worked it between us. Had a talk about old friends and schoolboys. Read a good piece called *The Grave*. Mr. Harris brought some spirits of wine and horse medicine from Cordwins and something from Woods. Didn't get in pit till just 12 p.m.

Left at ten to one a.m. Home at 2 a.m. Took two eggs. Sat up in chair to be ready for morning. Slept till 5.20 a.m.

Saturday Decr. 21st 1872

Pay day. At Trafalgar at 6.10 a.m. Ned Pollin and John Cooper took place in pit. [They] started this day. Received £2/3/6 wages for fortnight. Tried to bargain for leggings of John Mason.

Mr W.B.B. came into stores in morning and enquired if any parcels had been left there for him. Expected a parcel of valuables. Told him what had been. Received orders to go to Cinderford, Newnham and Lydney, to see if anything was there. Told me he would pay all expenses.

Left Trafalgar at 3 p.m. Home at 4 p.m. Tea, cleaned and started to Cinderford station. Received the largest parcel, 9 lbs, there. Rode to Newnham with the Bullo engine[118] and Ted Wilks. Paid for two quarts of ale, 8d. Had some gin put in it. Wilks came with me to Newnham station. Paid for four glasses and one quart of ale, 11d. Left parcels there at station.

Went to Gloster. Ticket 11d. Got into conversation with a lady,

'Started from Lydney at 2.30 a.m.'

Mrs. Humble of Clapham, London. Came to see a Dr. Collins of Newnham, her mother-in-law being there insane and the Collins' thereby receiving £250 a year instead of Mrs. Humble. Very nice spoken lady; had a little girl about seven with her. Told her I thought I could refer her to someone who was acquainted with the law and would probably give her some profitable advice.[119] Showed her Dauncevs Hotel. Went up street. Bought Beck a respirator, 5/–. Bought toffey 3d. for Peter's baby. Peter not at home, gone to Badgeworth for skates. Told Bessy my errand. She promised to send Peter down in the morning. Went to Wootton at 10 to 10 p.m. Beck came to door. Told her 'twas the bobby.

December 1872

Left at 11 p.m. and went to station. Jack Lewis nearly drunk. Morse came on platform. Saw Ben. Paid for one quart of ale and 6d. worth of pork pie. Did not stay long to speak with Morse. Poor Morse thinks I want to shun him.

Telegraphed Lydney, got no answer. Ticket 11d. to Newnham. Had parcels put in there and took ticket on to Lydney, 8½d. Looked over all parcels in the office. Started from Lydney at 2.30 a.m. Rode by the mail cart to Coleford. Walked mile or two up

'Rode by the mail cart to Coleford.'

hills. Stroking horse got bit on the finger. Gave the man 1/10½d. for ride. He knew all my old schoolfellows at Monmouth. Went to Bradshaw school. Told me Bob Webb dined with the Lord Mayor of London a short time hence.

Rained all the way from Lydney hard, and all the way from Coleford to Cinderford. Got very wet, and the parcels also. Got to Trafalgar at 6.30 a.m. Tom Jayne in engine house. Left parcels with him for Mr. W.B.B. Told him how wet I was and where I had been and that I hadn't been to bed since Thursday night.

'He knew all my old school-fellows at Monmouth.' *Monnow Street, Monmouth, where Bill Williams lived and went to school as a boy.*

[On way home from Trafalgar] slept walking along the road till I walk'd in the ditch. Then turned back, thinkingly to the road, and goes backward before discovering I was going wrong. Home at 7 a.m. Had cup of water and bit of bread and few sprats. Nearly famished out, and the sweetest meal I ever had. And very wet and very tired.

After arriving home I went to bed, slept till 5 p.m., then got up and done justice to a good roast beef dinner. Told adventures. Worth a sovereign.

Total spent 12/3d., ticket for concert 1/–: 13/3d.

Sunday Decr. 22nd

Bed all day. Got up at 5 p.m. Posted up diary. Tonic sol-fa'd a bit, not much. Took dinner and tea together. Talked a little. Bed again at 11 p.m.

Monday Decr. 23rd 1872

Dreamed a queer dream that Mrs. Green came to my bed and rode me and that her husband lay sleeping in next room and heard us. I thought he cut [illegible] Mrs. Green's throat and partly cut his own. Challenged me to fight. I accepted and he just disappeared. 'Twas a strange [dream], I thought. I think it's an evil forboding, will watch it out. Awoke in quite a simmer, with alarm. I suppose it will originate through Maria.

Received 13/– from Smith and 4d. owing and gave a pencil receipt for it. Mr. William B. Brain sent word for me to come up to give account of my adventures on Saturday night. Told him. Thanked me and said he was much obliged for my trouble, and Mr. Walter would pay my expenses on behalf of the firm.

Was informed that I had been shook for in W. Harris' raffle. Paid him 1/–. Pogson shook for me. Did not know I was in it. Was never ask'd about it. Mr Walter told me he would pay me 3/4d. on the morrow. Run quite out of oil.

Left Trafalgar at 5 p.m. Paid Greening 10/–, 18/– left. Bought two cakes 2d., three children's watches 8d. Bought papers 9d., diary 1/–, gloves for Maria 2/3d., pin cushion and needle book 10d., ticket for Mrs. Davis' tea party 1/–. Spent 6/8d.

Home just before 6 p.m. Wrote just a line to Maria wishing compliments of season. Bed at 11.15 p.m.

17/8d.

Tuesday Decr. 24th 1872

Rolled up at 5.40 a.m., at Trafalgar at 6.30 a.m. C.C.B. and I had a sore fall out about the Quabbs offal. Told me I was exceeding my duty. I told him different. Told Mr. William Brain the upshot and stated my grievance. He told me I was quite right and not to trouble about it, and that he thought of making alterations in his staff. Also told me to be just as strict with regard to everything else. Wrote to Mr. Jones, Lydney Carrying Company, to send the oil up. Been using olive oil and tar all day instead of vegetable oil.

'Had one glass of ale at Lower George.' *Newnham. The Lower George is on the left.*

Left Trafalgar at 4.30 p.m. Came home. Bill and Jim just gone to meet Sam [Bennett]. Came back, Jim a-swearing, Bill hoping his legs might drop off if ever he goes to meet him again. I went to Newnham Station to seek him. Failed. Called at the first public houses I saw likely in town to find him. Thought he may have been book'd for the night at Newnham. Had one glass of ale at *Lower George*, went to *Station*, had one glass there, and paid for one, 3d. Came back to the *George* at Newnham, had two glasses whiskey, 8d. Up in the town bought two lemons and two oranges, 1/9d. Bought bottle of whiskey at James', 2/9d. Total spent 4/6d. Composed a bit of music coming up from Newnham. Thought if I study I can get on with it. Home at 11.30 p.m. Talked a bit. Bed at 12.30.

Decr. 25th 1872 Xmas day

Rose late, about 10 a.m. Sam Bennett there before I rose. Self took breakfast with him. He had been taken wrong route and was taken to Hereford instead of Newnham. Brought Mrs. Green her lamp and slippers, &c. Lots about singing. Bill and Jim [Green] off first thing with the band. Came back, slept and dozed till evening. Was sent for by Morgan, Carrier. Bill, I and Jim went. Self took concertina and played with Bill a few waltzes, polkas and country dances. Kissed the girls under the mistletoe, sung and revelled till after 11 p.m. Return'd home and got singing till 1 a.m. Bed.

Thursday Decr. 26th 1872

Rose up at 8 a.m., at Trafalgar by 8.40 a.m. Pit working only one turn. Pogson not here. Saw Mr. W.B.B. in upper office, muttered something like compliments of season, did not hear distinctly what was said. W.B.B. trying [electrical] experiments on the wall with powder. Mr. Walter lost specimens of insulated wire. Found them in John Mason's sample bag, or rather paper bag. Jenkins nor Mason not at work. Mr. T.B. Brain in upper office at 3.30 p.m. Wished him the compliments of the season. Returned the same to me. Sent forty sacks off for corn. Took two bundles of sacks to the Bilson tip. Gave them in Bluett's charge.

Home about 4.30 p.m. Miss Wadley, Miss Morgan and Polly there waiting for me to come home. Got Polly into back room and got between her legs. Seemed to want it badly. No chance to accommodate.

Was asked to go down to Mitcheldean in Morgan's van. Didn't care to go, but went out for a walk with Sam Bennett. Told him about Mrs. Green and all the rest. Poor Sam was cut up. Took two glasses of whiskey and Bill and Jim [Green] took the same. Gave Oliver [Green] a ticket to go to Christy Minstrels, 1/–. One of Butterworth's Christies Minstrells died suddenly this morning. Didn't go to Mrs. Davis's tea party. Bill and I played violin and concertina last thing for Sam Bennett. Self gave each one glass of whiskey and lemon. Doubled Sam's whilst he was looking round.

Was rather afraid Sam would out with the secret. Promised to correspond. Poor Sam shook his head at me. Bed at 12 p.m.

Friday Decr. 27th 1872

Shied up at 5.35 a.m. Mr. W.B.B. trying experiments all the morning. John Mason and Harry Jenkins come, told me about their Christmas. Pogson busy along. Did no posting up all day. Fearful long way behind. Thought about Sam Bennett's promise to get me situation. Will keep silent respecting it. Told Jenkins about it. Sam Bennett went about 3 p.m. in afternoon. Chaffed Jane. Got close between her legs, gave me cock stand awfully.

Left Trafalgar at 5 p.m. Read *Wedding Bells* a little. Practised concertina two hours. Sat and rested. Nothing appeared to have been mentioned about what I told Sam. Very glad to find it so. Bed at 10 p.m.

Saturday Decr. 28th 1872

Up at Trafalgar by 6 a.m. Very wet and miserable. Rained hard all day. Dan Pogson at Trafalgar, then W.B.B. and Pogson making batteries for blasting by electricity. Carried them down to house and put them in billiard room. Bob Gwatkin and Ben Bennett assisted.

Left Trafalgar at 3 p.m. Bought *Reynold's* paper, received one from Beck. Home, read and cut out pieces for scrap book. Did not paste in any, and thought a good deal about Bennett's promise. Commenced to write him but failed and put it up for another day. Bed at 12 p.m.

Sunday Decr. 29th 1872

Shied up at 10. Arranged box. Did not clean for going out all day. Changed shirt in afternoon. Practised with violin and concertina in afternoon. Practised on tonic sol-fa a good while. Wrote Beck and started on a letter for Sam Bennett. Left off at commencement till Monday. Wrote the anthem *How Beautiful upon the Mountains*. Took minced pie for supper. Bed at 10.30 p.m.

busy along did no posting up all day
fearful long way behind thought abt S. B's promise
to get me situation, will keep silent respecting it
told Jenkins abt it – S.B went abt 3 pm in
Aft. noon, left Trafalgar at 5 pm Chaffd Jane
+
read wedding bells a little practised Con
2 hours sat & rested nothing appeared
+ very glad to find it so
Bed at 10 pm +

Saturday Decr 28th 1872
Up at Trafalgar by 6 am very wet
& Miserable rained hard all day
left Trafalgar at 3 pm. Pogson at
Trafalgar there WBB & D Pogson making
batteries for blasting ~~pating~~ by Electricity
Carried them down to House & put them in
billiard room Bob Gratkin, & Ben Bennett
assisted + Bought Reynold's paper recd
one from BKK + Home read & cut out
pieces for scrap book. did not paste in

A page of the diary.

Monday Decr. 30th 1872

Shied up at 5.40 a.m., at Trafalgar by 6.10 a.m. Commenced posting up as fast as possible again. End of year. Received two parcels, box of knife cleaner and box of brass works connected with the Barleigh drill. Mr. Walter over. Mr. W.B.B. caught Jane and I larking, said it was dreadful. Jane ran away. Said she only came for the note. Mr. Werner told me the best thing I could do would be to go to Bristol. Said it would be a good chance if I thought of going to New Zealand.

Intended to write Sam Bennett. Wrote Beck and sent paper and almanack out of *Forrester*. Bought *Uncle Tom's Cabin* for Oliver [Green] to read. Maria sent two cigars and box of fuses[120] for me.

Spent 2/4d. including everything.

Tuesday Decr. 31st 1872

Last day of the year. Morning fearfully rough. Cold and boisterous. Cleared up about 10 a.m. Got very wet going to work. Bought off John Mason a new pair of leggings, india rubber, 7/–. Posted up as much of old arrears as possible. Middle of day nice and fine.

Worked for Smith second turn. Book'd the majority of men out of pit by 12 a.m. midnight. Made new intentions for the new year. Leant on desk and prayed for divine assistance through coming year, and resolved on starting future efforts with a good will, grappling with God's favour against inclination, flesh and world, and leaning more faithfully and resignedly on His Omnipotent Arm, bidding cares avaunt and pushing forward cheerfully and hopefully.

Home at 1.30 p.m. midnight. Bells were ringing the new year in. Received letter from poor Beck. Read it, enjoyed supper over it very much. Bed. Slept well.

END OF 1872

Doctor Young expressing the grief of surviving relatives thus –

When such friends part ''tis the survivors die'

Ode

Man, thoughtless man! whose moments quickly fly,
Wakes but to sleep again, and lives to die.
And, when this present fleeting life is o'er
Man dies to live, and lives to die no more.

From now on there is not an entry for every day and Bill clearly writes up several days at once.

Sunday Jany. 5th 1873

Took dinner with Beck. Left her about 2 p.m. Went to Isaiah Morse's, poor fellow. Knew me in a moment and told me to be cautious and that he would rather die than anyone else should catch it [smallpox].[121] Sat on his bed and talked whilst he was conscious, wandering very much. Dr. Campbell came at 9.30 p.m., chatted a good while. Mr. Kell said his treatment was atrocious to Mr. Morse. I asked doctor what he considered his time to come. Told me every other day. Mr. Kell very nervous, said he would leave in the morning. Dr. Campbell did laugh. Told me there was no fear of my taking it the second time. Prayed for poor Morse deeply.

Mrs. Morse begged me to try and come and stay for a week. Promised my wages should be made good. Told her I would ask Mr. Brain for leave for a week. Oh, how relieved poor Ellen [Morse] felt after. Called up Mr. Hacker at 12 a.m. to come and stop with poor Morse.

Left per mail [train], drank glass of whiskey at Gloster Hotel. Left umbrella at Gloster Hotel. Saw poor Jack Lewis at Gloster. Had good long chat. Told him about Morse. Gent lying dead in W.C. room waiting. Had company to Littledean. Home at 3 a.m. Had apple pie and two glasses beer. Bed.

Monday Jany. 6th 1873

Couldn't turn poor Morse off my mind. Tried to see Mr. Brain for to get leave off. Couldn't get opportunity. Wrote to Mrs. Morse telling her I would endeavour to come if I didn't telegraph. Wrote to Beck. Did not post Beck's letter.

Tuesday

Received letter from Beck. Wrote a reply to it against I arrived in Gloster. Promised to put the time on that I posted it, and did so. Saw Mr. W.B.B. Told him the circumstances and appealed to him for absence for a short time, or a few days at most. He promised me if my work could be arranged till my return I should go. Self arranged with Chappell and Smith to work till I returned. Wrote W.B.B. from the weighbox (being at work Tuesday night). Told him everything was complete but his sanction. Mr. Walter sent word to say he would call upon me. Called in about a quarter of an hour at weighbox and asked how long I should be away. Told him probably a week or till a nurse could be obtained. Didn't give any stated time. Request granted. Worked Tuesday night in weighbox. Delivered up keys to Chappell at 6 a.m. in morning.

Wednesday

Home. Went to bed till 2 p.m. Prepared for start. Packed up all necessaries. Bought box 2d., bottle of brandy 3/1d., heavy load of clothes &c. Mrs. Green sent small pot of black currant jam. Took six or eight kerchiefs for immergency.

Arrived at Gloster about 8 p.m. Bought a shillings worth of oranges, chloride of something 6d., camphor 6d., new hat 4/6d. Gave Annie Gentle 1/–. Took books for poor Morse to read. He had been calling all the time since Sunday for Bill. Went to 3 Stapleton Place [Morse's house]. Saw Mrs. Kell. Were all quite pleased to see me. Mrs. Morse thought of telegraphing for me, but depended on my word. Fare 1/– for the journey. Changed and sent clothes to old Mr. Hacker.

Poor Morse impatient to see me, called me his dear old friend. Felt quite melted to see the poor fellow in such a prostrate and helpless condition. Helped him out of bed twice on Wednesday night. Thought he was going on very favourable. Delirious part of his time.

'Went to 3 Stapleton Place.' *Stapleton Place, Ryecroft Street, Gloucester, today.*

Thursday

Morning fine and warm. Poor Morse very prostrate and ill, wanted attention every minute. Went and examined his legs and feet. Did not like the symptoms at all. Told Mrs. Morse. She begged of me to go and see Dr. Campbell. Mr. Doctor was very sharp and purgry to me, didn't half like it. Talked to him and cooled him down. He told me to go and make him comfortable and give him plenty of beef tea, milk and eggs and nourishments.

Went home and met Rowland [Morse] at the door with tears in his eyes. He told me he was almost cut up. Had been to see Morse. Told me he never wanted to see small pox again. Morse said he thought it was all over. Rowland said he thought so, too. I told him no and also what Dr. Campbell had told me and quite cheered up all of us.

Put Morse comfortable and talked to him. Told him what doctor had said. Soaked his eyes in afternoon and opened them.

He saw Mrs. Morse and me and blessed us and was so pleased and thought he was getting better. Was very conscious all day. Spoke of some of the railway officials at intervals when delirious. In trouble on all sides. Begged of me to go and fetch Tom Hacker to come and shake hands with him so that they may feel at peace with each other.

Morse felt so happy after Tom went. Began to grow very restless on Thursday evening. I was changing him nearly all night. Ate and drank all day quite vigourously. Washed ten napkins for him on Thursday night. Self felt nervous upon times.

Somewhat timid old woman (Tyler) [a nurse] slept well. Room very strongly pregnated from the fever. I was obliged to wear flannel bags with camphor over the mouth all or most of the time.

Mrs. Morse went to bed and slept for the first time since Isaiah's illness, thinking he was going on well. Poor Morse told me he was going a journey, going Home. He asked me if I was coming. Told him he was at home. He says, 'No Bill, I am not,' but he was going and would not wait for me. Felt deeply all poor Morse's words. They were so thoughtfull and serious. They told but too plain of his departure for another clime. He could see far beyond here, but we were blind to that. Poor Morse, how tiresome and tedious the night rolled by, like so many seasons of the year, so slow, so long. Poor Morse thought it weeks.

Friday

I felt thankful for the dawn. Poor Morse was very anxious for to know the day and the time to a minute. Said on Wednesday he shouldn't go today. On Friday morning poor Morse look'd very deathly, moaned very much, called 'Ellen' several times. I sent Mrs. Morse a cup of tea about 5 a.m. Morse called 'Ellen' very loud and distinct. Mrs. Morse answered him, and I went and told him poor Ellen was asleep. He said let her stop, then fell into a tiresome sleep. Did not wake, placed himself in various positions, breathed for three hours as if in great pain, then shorter and harder for some time, afterwards to a short, soft, peaceful sleep.

LEE'S FUNERAL FURNISHING ESTABLISHMENT,

The Best and Cheapest in the City, as the following prices will show :—

	£	s.	d.
Funeral, with Hearse and Coach, with pair of Horses and Hanging Velvets to each; four Bearers, Coffin covered with Black Cloth, richly Nailed, best Metal Plate, lined with Flannel, Flannel Dress, Pall, Cloaks, Hatbands, and Attendance within three miles of the City	**5**	0	0
Second Class, also Black Cloth	4	0	0
Third Class, with French-Polished Coffin, or Black Cloth, and Appendages as above	3	0	0

Hearses for the removal of corpses, within three miles of the City, 5s., or any part of the United Kingdom, at 1s. per mile.

Pair-Horse Hearse, or Mourning Coaches, supplied to any distance, at 2s. per mile, beyond ten miles of the City, including every expense.

Morris & Co.'s Commercial Directory of Gloucestershire, 1865–66.

'Made every arrangement for poor Morse's interment: a one horse hearse and one mourning coach.'

Never spoke after sleep commenced. About 11 a.m. I ran down and fetched Mrs. Morse to come and see him. She advised me to go for doctor. Nurse said not as it was all useless. Took Mrs. Morse downstairs, ran up again but only for a few seconds. Ran down once again. Poor Ellen said my step, my look, told her the last sad tale. She ask'd what was the upshot. I said, 'All's well, poor Isaiah has taken his last farewell for a fairer region than this'——

The blow was hard to Mrs. Morse, but quite expected. It was not at all like snow in harvest. She was quite resigned and met her blow bravely.

Went and obtained Mrs. Morse's money and certificates and registered. Received letter from poor Beck. Mrs. Kell going up to tell her the circumstances and suddenness of the occurence. Ordered coffin.

Mr. Hacker was coming home just as I was going to fetch him. He was struck when I told him the news. Saw Mr. Kell at the railway gates, told him the sad news. He was almost bewildered. Ask'd me to come and take a glass of brandy. Went into the *Bell Inn*, the first time since Jack Lewis and I was there between four and five years hence.

Dr. Campbell said he was very sorry and wrote his certificates out for two clubs and Registrar and a certificate stating that I had been nursing a friend. Promised to come and see Mrs. Morse as soon as he could. Made every arrangement for poor Morse's interment: a one horse hearse and one mourning coach. Laid him out and washed him with help of Mrs. Tyler. Oh! irksome task. And yet a duty.

But it gave true satisfaction. I felt more than happy withall. Self buried and burnt everything that had been among the fever. Cut off a bit of poor Isaiah's hair, kept a little myself. Labelled envelopes.

Mr. Charles Morse came from Sellesley[122] to No. 3 Stapleton Place on the night of the death. Look'd quite pleased and seemed as if going to spend a convivial evening instead of the funeral of a poor son. Mrs. Morse quite hurt at his demeanour.

Slept at Mr. Hacker's on Friday, Saturday and Sunday.

Saturday

Went home to fetch black clothes.

Sunday

Saw Beck on Sunday night. I went to go to the Allington School to go and fetch her. She was just gone to Corn Exchange. I stopped and talk'd with Mary instead of going away. She expected Beck about 8 p.m. Didn't come. Self left Wootton about quarter to 10 p.m. Met my lady coming home alone. I turned back [with her]. She was very much hurt at Morse's death. I stopped till after prayers, then caressed my own a short time. Bade her Adieu for a good while with a promise to write shortly.

Did in about a week. Told her all I could about poor Isaiah. Received no answer for a week. Very kind letter from Beck teling me that Mary was going to leave and going to keep house for somebody else who was a widower. Heard from Rowland Morse same day.

Friday Jany 24th 1873

Mr. W.B.B. intimated a change of post to me. Told me it was not out of the slightest disrespect to me, but that he regarded Smith with a little jelousy.[123] But wished me to inform him if anyone offered me a bribe or any temptation. Promised him I would.

Mr. Chappel had been making a little mischief. A party, Jim Brain, told me he heard that H. Chappell had told his uncle I was rather dull[124] in office. I knew something like mischief has been going on, for W.B.B. told me that there would be lots of things missing if I left sudden that I should be quite innocent of.

Felt quite perplexed about the week closing so unsatisfactory. Forgot all about Christ takes my weary heart to Him and finds relief —— thought much of poor Morse.

Sunday night Jany. 26th

Dreamt that I was going down the pit and that one of the ears of the carriage had broken and the carriage stopped in the middle of the pit. The rope ran by very fast and the carriage hung there.

Cinderford High Street

Couldn't make anyone hear on top. Could not show a signal. All of us felt ourselves in the jaws of death.

Couldn't sleep again. Sweat very much, so terrified. Related all my distress to Jesus. Felt relieved. And slept after well. Thought of poor Morse's hymn, *I always go to Jesus*. Never felt experimentally the real peace afforded from simply casting all upon the Man of Sorrows who still intercedes for weary and distressed ones. Can never again forget the receipt for a sleepless night ——

Sunday Feby. 2nd 1873

R.R. Handy slept with me. Rose about 9.10 a.m. Could not get in time for Chapel. Prees still ill.[125] Sat with choir. No school in afternoon. Very few in Chapel both morn and evening, only three singers there. After Chapel went and spent an hour with R.R. Handy at the Temperance House. Felt quite interested in him and sorry for him. He offered to take me out to America.

February 1873

Handy is a most deep, learned, intelligent man, bred among the highest of the high. Been captain in 45th Regiment foot, very proud and haughty in his air, but thorough repentant for his misdemeanour. Has his annuity divided between himself and wife, £100 each. Never goes to his father's house, Park House, county of West Meath, Ireland. His father is a Justice of the Peace and a Grand Juror of the County of West Meath – income £3,000 per annum or over. Handy is very drunken and dissipated, very poor. W.B.B. pays him 3/– per day, daily. So sorry to see a man of his birth and education in such a deplorable situation. He belongs to the order of Free Masons. Wishes me to become a member and would have proposed me had he been staying in the Forest. His profession is that of landscape gardener. He is a most ingenious and talented man and great admirer of nature and beauty. Mr. W.B.B. has employed him about three weeks. Cannot continually employ him. W.B.B. gave him 1£ extra to help him on further till his annuity becomes due. Promised to write to me before he goes to America.

Market Street, Cinderford

Saturday Feby. 8th 1873

Gave up the charge of the stores at Trafalgar. Very glad to have done with it. Going to take charge of weighing and booking down the men, sheets &c. Will make fresh start at phonography now. Will take books on Monday.

Sunday Feby. 9th 1873

Spent {day} badly, fearful of a bad start on Monday. Pretty good after {I started} – see daily diary.

Bill now keeps two diaries: this one, in which he makes entries usually only on Sundays and in which he concentrates mainly on his religious thoughts; and a new one, which he calls his daily diary and which he devotes to more mundane happenings during the week. The new one is lost. It may have been in the old trunk from which Gregory Jones rescued this diary.

A change has clearly come over him. He is unsettled because his plans to emigrate are not progressing, and short of money because the colliery is not working full time. Further, his lifestyle has altered: he changes his lodgings, spends his time with different people and attends different places of worship. More significantly, he becomes a teetotaller and is absorbed by religion.

Sunday Feby. 16th 1873

Refused pudding for dinner. Mrs Green awfully put about over my moving place. Commented a good while with a lot of insolence. <u>Took no notice</u>. Enquired once if she was addressing me or who. No answer.

After dinner Mrs. Green asked me what I meant by going, so told her that was my business, and needed no dictation upon it. She told me that I had asked Polly {Dykins} to leave her situation. I did ask Polly if she wanted a situation because a friend of mine at Gloster ask'd me to reccomend her a servant, and I thoughtlessly asked Polly what I did. Felt very much annoyed about it. Left box open whilst at Chapel. No doubt rummaged well over. Very vex'd and annoyed. Polly gets treated

Market Street, Cinderford.

cool on that account.

Good sermon preached at Baptist Chapel from *Acts of Apostles* XI chapter 22, 23, and 24th verses, a comparison of Mr. Preece with Barnabas going about his mission and showing the abilities of one with the other, Mr. Preece having been buried on Friday evening last. Very great respect paid him. A great many ministers there. Joined choir morn and night. Tremendous congregation. Mr. W.B.B. there, C.C.B. and Frank Brain. Passed by Mrs. Green.

Evening sermon very touching and instructive. Mr. Rhodes's letter from the Revd. Barker of Holy Trinity read to congregation. Text from 30th chapter *St. Luke*, 46th verse. Tom Call, tenor voice, joined Cinderford choir. Polly Dykins and Samuel Tyndall sat among the choir close to me. Bessy Morgan and Polly called on Mrs. Green after Chappel.

Bed at 9.30 p.m. No supper.

Thursday April 10th 1873

Reflecting on passed week spent idly. Tried a great many times to get an interview with Sleeman and probably a little advice that would be advantageous. Feel very disheartened. Cannot work with any pleasure at home.[126] No work for past week, and only nine turns for previous fortnight.[127] Went to Trafalgar each day with a view of working. No trade for second shift.[128] Strip[-and-at-it Pit] worked four turns.

Received one of the most kind letters from Beck I ever did on Tuesday last advising me to stay till end of summer and go over to America and Beck will come in spring of 1874.

Cinderford's Commercial Street (left) and Station Street (later called Victoria Street). The Baptist chapel can be seen in the distance along Commercial Street.

Sunday April 20th 1873

Delightful morning, never one more beautiful. Thoughts travelling back to years passed away. This morning dreamt that Beck had again met with Winter. I thought he shunned me and kept out of my sight, but Beck came boldly forward and told me she had made up all with her old lover. I observed there seemed something more defiant in her look than usual, and her sharp, piercing glance filled me with awe. I read in her features the consciousness of having broken her oath, and now there were two small wrinkles beside each eye that told of care or remorse or something unexplained. But I noticed them in particular. I bravely and calmly tendered her my hand and bade her goodbye. I felt sick and troubled. Awoke, 'twas 8 o'clock. Rose at once, cleaned boots, wash'd all over and breakfasted. Wrote shorthand short time.

Had frequent solicitations to go to Mrs. Goold's Wesleyan Chapel, the last sermon to be preached by Mr. Harris. Declined. Went to the little Chapel. Mr. Lane, a new minister, preached just the sermon. I enjoyed text from *Genesis* 32nd, verse 24 and three following. He spoke of the wrestling of nature at the Jabbock brook where Jacob wrestled with the Angel of the Lord and prevailed and would not let the Angel go untill he was blessed. . . . Mr. Lane compared the struggle against habit as a wrestler at the brook, giving a picture of the drunkard and his combat with the old practice. He also gave a picture of a widowed mother and starving family wrestling with poverty, and the business man who wrestles either by misfortune or misadventure. The proffessional, the learned, the soldier, the sailor, the illiterate, every one of us have to take our share in the conflict – if not with the Angel [as] Jacob did, [then] with a substitute – to test and prove us as the Angel had proved Jacob e'er he was deemed worthy of the blessing and new name. And Mr. Lane showed that our trials and tears here were in reality blessings, secret blessings. He gave instruction and encouragement to the young, the parents and aged.

Mr. Lane made a good mark of his commencement. Hymn 140th, tune *Stella*.

After Chapel went into enclosure[129] and wrote above. Home at 1 p.m., dined, out again for a walk and for a view of Gloster, enjoying own thoughts, thinking of last Sunday, and the wrestle against nature both by Beck and self. Thinking I am got very wicked since poor Morse went into his rest. Seem to have lost the way or gone back with Timorous instead of plodding toward the Cross.

Heavenly evening, thought only Beck was wanted to share that delightful walk between the banks to complete <u>happiness</u>.

Stayed in after 4 p.m., read, wrote Beck very long letter, wrote shorthand, put tea for myself. Out little toward 8 p.m. Meditating good deal all day.

Sunday April 27th 1873

Rolled out about 9 a.m. James Griffiths[130] set off at 5 a.m., not home to breakfast. Self cleaned, went to Wesleyan Chapel. Sat with George Gwilliam. Very poor preacher. Couldn't remember text, not interested in it at all. Collection, gave 6d. Talked few minutes with Gwilliam. Went up street with a few Good Templars[131] and requested to join Society. Agreed. Going to converse with a member, the Rev. Lane, who holds a dignified office therein.

After dinner went out to Amos Hale's. Wrote *Lady Prince's* tune for him in *Bristol Tune Book*. James and Miss Landen took tea and dined together. After tea went to town hall to hear Mr.

'Went to Town Hall to hear Mr. Marquand.' *Town Hall, Cinderford, in the 1870s*

Marquand of Ross and met Mr. Werner and Mr. Jones of Pontypool, late engineer at Trafalgar. Offered me a post at 22/– per week. Couldn't accept it, declined with thanks.

Thought of what Mr. W.B.B. once told me with regard to Mr. Jones's being a mongrell. Wished Mr. Jones well and goodbye. Mrs. Burdess and daughter and son sat next me on adjoining chairs. Wondered if I shall work for them.

Mr. Marquand gave a brief address on the cause of being compelled to meet there in an unconsecrated sanctuary.

He chose a very appropriate and well-chosen text. . . . In the old Jewish dispensation, *II Chronicles* VI, we read of the appointed place for worship, viz. the holy mountain in the holy temple with faces turned Zionward. But Jesus told the woman of Samaria at Jacob's well that the hour cometh when you shall neither in this mountain nor yet at Jerusalem worship the Father. But the hour cometh when the true worshipper shall worship the Father in spirit and in truth, for the Father seeketh to worship Him. And with reference to Church the sanctuary matters not. The sanctuary is not God's church, but the two or three in unity and spirit are the Church. Accepted.

[Mr. Marquand] gave vent in brief to their sorrow in parting with their Chapel but hoped their bonds would be strengthened, and that many would join them and they would warmly recieve all. Hymn 635–625 *Stella*.

Sunday May 4th 1873

Rose at 6.20 a.m. Washed all over. Wrote a note to W.B.B. declining his proffered favour, viz. to return for a week or two or month or two or regular if I liked at same rate of wages, reminding him of my susceptabillity of his good feeling towards me &c. Played short time with Cook. Went round the hill for a walk, James [Griffiths] and self. Spoke to James about borrowing £1/–/– for a week. Promised it. Came home, took mackerul for breakfast and eggs.

Went to Wesleyan Chapel. Sat by poor George Gwilliam. Mr. Lane preached from XI *Proverbs* and part of 30th verse, 'And he that winneth souls is wise.' He commented at length upon Solomon's wisdom and celebrated writings, his volumes of philosophy, his talent, judgement, qualities and lastly his depravity – in our own fallen nature. None perfect. No, not one. Most affectionate and kind sermon, but not the most instructive I had heard.

Walk'd in wood before dinner. Wrote a little after dinner, posting up diary. Slept a short time. Tea at 5 p.m. James out.

After tea walked down to George Gwilliam. Both went to town hall. Mr. Lane preached very interesting sermon with much warmth and evidently affected. The room well filled with (apparently) an earnest congregation. Took his text from *St. Mathew* 25th chapter upon the ten virgins. Gave a graphic description of the old eastern custom, the midnight procession, the sounding tomtoms, the order of the procession throughout, the great cry of 'Behold! The bridegroom cometh. Go ye out to meet him,' the surprise of the sleeping virgins, the panic among the foolish five virgins whose lamps were gone out, their dismay, their terror.

He handled it with telling impressions and fervently, with appropriate anecdotes and sincere exhortations to bring about a revival. He referred to their presumption on Mercy and the tremulous knock at the door and also their denial, animadverting on the conduct of the five foolish maidens and corresponding them with the foolish of the present day.

Beautiful hymns were sang, and a choice prayer offered by one of the congregation and the benidiction pronounced by Mr. Lane.

Out early, went for short walk with Mr. Gwilliam. Asked in after service. Was invited to tea there. Couldn't stop. Home. Wrote notes of sermon. Read Proverbs. Prayers. Thought of Beck. James not in by 10 p.m. Mr. and Mrs. Avott left me writing ——

Here ends Bill's diary. For some weeks he seems to have lost interest in everyday happenings and people. Hitherto self-assured, he is now uncertain of himself and has become depressed. He has left his job at Trafalgar and refused William Brain's offer to employ him again, though why he will not go back we do not know, for he is short of cash. He has become obsessed with religion. It is difficult to suggest a reason for these changes; perhaps the death of his friend Morse at the beginning of the year upset him more than one would expect, or perhaps his state was due to his inability to find a suitable job.

Nor can we discover what happened to him after he stopped keeping his diary. No trace of him in the Forest can be found; the records in New Zealand of the men who went there with Brogdens do not include his name; there is no evidence that he went to America; and no record has been discovered that he married Beck.

Bill just slips away as quietly as he came to our notice when his diary was discovered in that old trunk.

Appendix

More about Trafalgar Colliery, Cinderford Baptist Chapel and People Mentioned in the Diary

Trafalgar Colliery was galed – leased from the Crown – in 1842 by Cornelius Brain, the father of William and Thomas Brain, but coal was not mined there until about 1860. The colliery remained in the possession of the Brain family until 1921. It closed in 1925.

In its day it was one of the biggest and most up-to-date collieries in Dean. It was the first to use electricity underground. In 1867 an electrically operated communication system was introduced to ensure the safe operation of the engine drawing the loaded carts from the workings to the bottom of the pit shaft – the dipple engine that Bill refers to. There was also an electrical communications system with the surface. Later, electricity was introduced for lighting, pulling trucks underground, pumping water and winding coal and men up the pit shaft. This was in the 1880s, but we know that there was an electrical machine of some sort at Trafalgar in Bill's day, because he tells us he couldn't get it to work.

Trafalgar was also the first pit to use electricity for blasting. It was probably also the first to use gas for lighting underground – naked flames were possible in Dean's pits because there was no danger of explosion from fire damp. A newspaper report tells us that in 1874 some visitors to Trafalgar were surprised to discover that the roadways underground were lit by gas. But Bill refers to gas experiments, the gas man and gas shortages in 1872. The colliers did not think much of the gas lighting – they still needed to use candles at the coal face and resented having the cost of the gas deducted from their wages.

THE TRAFALGAR COLLIERY, FOREST OF DEAN.

On Friday afternoon last a visit was made to this well-known colliery by Captain and Mrs. Wanys and party, of the Wilderness, near Mitcheldean, who, in company with Mr. T. B. Brain, descended the shaft in the ordinary skiff. In this subterranean passage the visitors had not calculated upon finding the roadway lighted with gas, similar to that employed in the lighting of streets and dwellings, and were greatly surprised to find, instead of impenetrable darkness, the workings clearly defined from the jet burners which were dotted about the roadway. After a further investigation of the pit, the return journey was made shortly before the day men ascended for the evening shift to take their places at three o'clock. It may be of interest to add that the gas is forced down the shaft by means of a one-horse horizontal engine erected in the gas house on the pit bank.

Gloucester Journal, *30 October 1874.*

Though it was an up-to-date colliery, in the 1870s it harboured constant industrial unrest. The first coal miners' strike in Dean was at Trafalgar in 1871. It was successful and led to other strikes at other collieries, and a miners' union was formed in the area shortly afterwards. The union improved colliers' pay and reduced their working hours throughout the Forest, but its success was shortlived. In 1874 the employers tried to reduce colliers' pay by 25 per cent; the union opposed them and they had to be satisfied with 10 per cent. A few months later they tried again and, after a bitter strike, succeeded in not only imposing a further 5 per cent reduction, but crushing the trade union as well. The Brains played their part in all this.

William Blanch Brain – W.B.B. – was the leading member of the two-man team at Trafalgar. His brother, *Thomas Bennett Brain*, though ten years older, often found himself in the background and there was sometimes tension between the two of them. W.B.B. certainly pushed on with things. He was married at nineteen – his wife was then fifteen or sixteen – and they had eleven children.

As well as taking the major part in running the colliery, he experimented with making electrical fuses to detonate the explosives used for blasting coal. The Electric Blasting Apparatus Company resulted. The company's dynamo-magnetos and the Brain fuses they exploded were successfully used in collieries, quarries and other industrial sites, both inside and outside the Forest, for many years.

The Brain brothers had financial troubles in the late 1870s and early '80s. These were caused to a large extent by a lawsuit against them for allowing water from two of their pits to encroach on neighbouring pits. The Court awarded £20,000 against them. A family quarrel followed, with the result that in 1885 W.B.B. emigrated to Australia with most of his family. He died in New Zealand in 1908.

Frank Brain was sixteen when he was taken on at Trafalgar in 1872. He assisted W.B.B. with his explosive experiments and later took over the Electric Blasting Apparatus Company that W.B.B. had started. He also carried out pioneer work elsewhere in the commercial use of electricity. In 1879, by installing floodlighting at the site of the railway bridge then being built across the Severn near Lydney, he enabled work to be carried out at night, a novel achievement. In 1882, with W.B.B., he introduced electricity underground at Trafalgar for pumping and winding, the first ever use of electricity for these purposes.

Frank also worked on the colliery side. Early in his career he became a pit manager, and later he was made a partner. He moved into Trafalgar House in 1880 and stayed there for the next thirty-five years. When W.B.B. fled to Australia in 1885, Frank took over as sole owner of the colliery. He became a Fellow of the Institute of Civil Engineers, President of the Association of Colliery Managers and President of the Mining Association of Great Britain, and in 1913 he was knighted. He died in 1921.

William J. Smith was perhaps the Smith with whom Bill had so many arguments. He was about nineteen when Bill was employed at Trafalgar. By 1878 he was working with Frank Brain in his experiments in electricity and electric shot firing for

180 CINDERFORD ADVERTISEMENT.

THE

Electric Blasting Apparatus

COMPANY,

CINDERFORD, FOREST OF DEAN, GLOUCESTERSHIRE.

A SMALL DYNAMO-MAGNETO,

As made by Messrs. Siemens Bros., price £25., will explode 1,000 of Brain's High Tension Fuses simultaneously.

WHERE SUCCESSFULLY USED—

Lydney Harbour, by Mr. Holbrough, Contractor.

Sharpness Point Docks, by Mr. Holbrough, Contractor.

Nerquis Colliery, near Mold, by the Proprietors.

Hawkwell Colliery, Forest of Dean, by the Proprietors.

White Oak Collieries, Nailsea, by the Burleigh Rock Boring Company, Limited.

Salford Sewerage Works, by Messrs. Worthington, Contractors.

Drybrook Iron Co., Limited, Drybrook, Forest of Dean, by the Proprietor.

Morris & Co.'s Commercial Directory of Gloucestershire, 1876. *Note the reference to Brain's High Tension Fuses.*

Sir Francis Brain in 1913

blasting, and in 1885 he became his partner. He died in 1895 at the age of forty-two.

John Mason, Bill's colleague and friend, started his working life as a letter carrier, at what age we don't know. We are told, however, that he began work at Trafalgar Colliery when he was eight. He was seventeen when Bill first met him. By the time he had reached his early thirties he had risen to the post of company cashier. He was a genial man who enjoyed the confidence of his employers and was much respected by his friends and neighbours.

His private life, however, was a sad one. At twenty-seven he married against the advice of his family. His wife bore him a daughter, but died three years after their wedding. The marriage was tragic; his wife squandered all his money, and even four years after her death he was engulfed by financial troubles caused by her extravagance. He had mortgaged his house for £150, borrowed £90 from his father and, as was to be discovered, had pilfered at least £200 from his employers. These were big sums in the 1880s.

The day before the auditors were due to come to audit the company's accounts in 1889, John came to the office and made up his books for the day. He said he would be at work the following morning at 7 a.m., but he failed to arrive. During the night he had committed suicide by drinking prussic acid. He was thirty-four. He had covered his intentions well, for no one – employers, friends or family – had suspected that he was contemplating such a step. His wife had left anguish in his heart, but in a suicide note he asked to be buried by her side.

Timothy Mountjoy was a well-known character in the Forest in the 1870s and '80s and is still remembered there with affection. A teetotaller and man of religion, he was also a strong advocate of fair shares and decent living standards for working people. He was a collier and helped to form the first miners' trade union in Dean. He stumped the Forest ceaselessly for many years, making long speeches in the course of his work for the union. Formal education he had little, getting only 'as far as multiplication at school', but he wrote an interesting autobiography called *Sixty-two Years in the Life of a Forest of Dean Collier*. In 1874 he gave evidence to a Select Committee of the House of Commons which had been set up to enquire into conditions in the Forest, especially into its collieries and its social and sanitary needs. Until he became a full-time trade union official Timothy worked for the Crawshays at their Lightmoor Colliery.

Edwin Crawshay and his father, Henry, were perhaps the biggest coal and iron masters in the Forest in the nineteenth century. Henry's father, William, had come to Dean in the 1830s from Merthyr Tydfil in Wales. His family had earlier established at Merthyr an enormous iron empire, the biggest in the world at the time. The Welsh Crawshays were hard employers and their ruthless dealings with their workers had been the main cause of the riots in Merthyr in 1831. Edwin and Henry, on the other hand, were fair masters, among the best in the Forest, popular with their employees and more considerate than the Brain brothers or the Goold brothers (one of whose dog followed Bill home). Consequently the Crawshays did not suffer from strikes and other labour problems to the extent that the others did. As well as owning many coal pits and iron mines, they owned the prosperous Cinderford ironworks, where Bill's room-mates, the Green boys, and their father worked.

Cinderford Baptist Chapel. Until 1843 the Baptists had met in the house of William Rhodes, Cinderford's postmaster. Then they built a chapel. However, this soon proved to be too small for their growing congregation and was replaced in 1860 by the present chapel. One can imagine Bill sitting in the gallery in his Sunday best, wearing a stiff celluloid collar, criticizing the sermons of the Revd Prees and keeping an eye open for the girls in the congregation.

William Frowan Rhodes, with whom Bill had altercations, was Cinderford's first postmaster. He opened the post office in his grocer's shop in about 1846, and his salary was £4 a year. Rhodes was a devout Baptist and was the senior deacon and treasurer of Cinderford Baptist Chapel. He died in 1884. His son, *Thomas Frowan Rhodes*, who succeeded him as postmaster, is also referred to in the diary.

The Revd Phillip Prees (whose name Bill usually spelt 'Preece') came from Wales. He was appointed pastor of Cinderford Baptist Chapel in 1858, and everyone spoke warmly of his devotion and zeal. Physically he was far from strong, though few people knew of his infirmities. Bill was not impressed by his sermons, but he knew Prees only in the last months of his life when he was clearly a sick man. He died in 1873 aged forty-one.

George Waite was, like William Rhodes, a grocer. He joined Cinderford Baptist Chapel when he moved to the town in 1854. He soon became a deacon and superintendent, supervising its adults' and children's classes, and was also its choirmaster. He died in 1893.

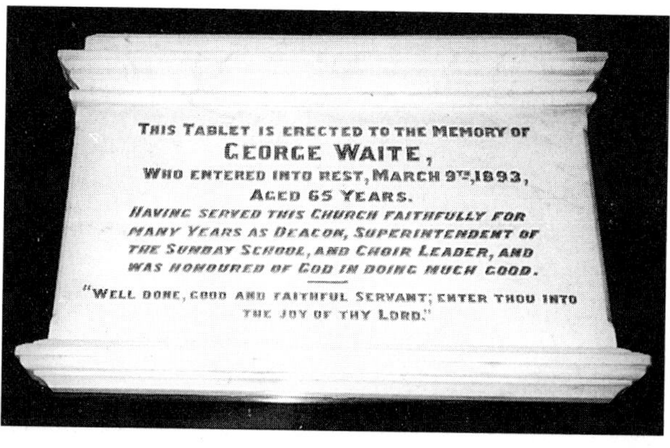

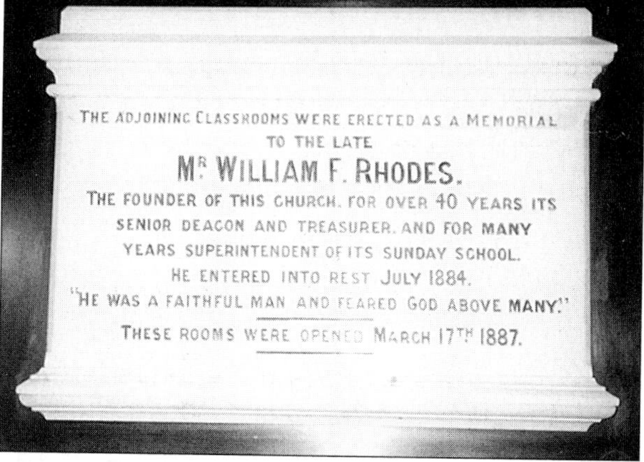

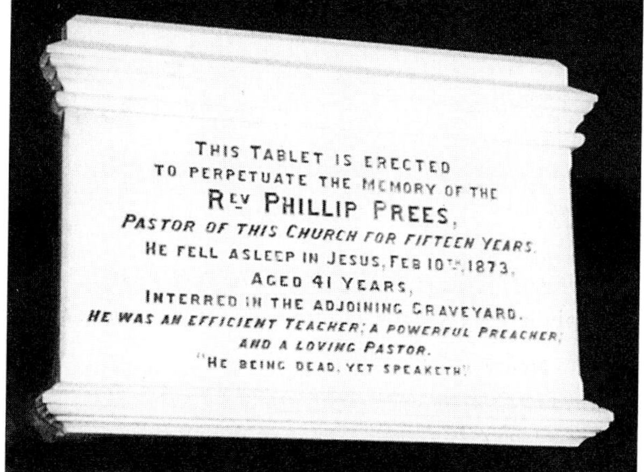

Memorial plaques in Cinderford Baptist Chapel.

Moses Boey was Cinderford's first postman

Moses Boey was Cinderford's first postman, and probably delivered Bill's letters. He began to work for William Rhodes as a young lad in about 1851. He rode round on his horse sounding his horn and people came to him to collect their mail. It was he who suggested to Rhodes and Prees, when they were bemoaning that the old chapel was too small to accommodate the ever-growing congregation, that they should buy the field next to it and build a new one. Rhodes clapped his hands, we are told, and said 'Good, Moses! A capital idea!' Prees was equally taken by the suggestion, but his reaction was more circumspect: he just nodded his approval.

Moses was asked, perhaps as a joke, how much he would give towards the purchase of the land. He said he would give £5, on condition that he was the first to be married in the new chapel. At the time he had no idea of getting wed, and had not even met the girl who eventually became his wife. Nevertheless, he was the first to be married in the new building. Moses was still alive in 1910.

Explanatory Notes

1 'Trafalgar Colliery play'd' means that the colliery was not working, on this occasion because of a strike.

2 Gardner Lewis was employed at Trafalgar on the gas installations.

3 There were two shafts at Trafalgar, about 35 yards apart, each 200 yards deep. Coal came up one shaft, empties went down the other. There was an office at the bottom where Bill worked when he was 'in pit'.

4 Beck (Rebecca Loveridge) was Bill's girlfriend.

5 Halliday was the president of the Amalgamated Association of Miners.

6 In later years Chappell became a bailiff (pit manager) at Trafalgar.

7 Ed Cooksey was a fellow employee.

8 Warry was a fellow employee.

9 McKuskey was a Polish Jew from Warsaw and a tailor. How he came to such a remote area as the Forest of Dean must be an intriguing story. He married a Cinderford woman and was later involved in a bigamy case.

10 It seems that the three Green sons, Jim, William and John, shared a bedroom with Bill, and sometimes one or the other of them also shared a bed with him.

11 'Bringing out tools' normally meant going on strike.

12 John Mason was a fellow employee.

13 Harry Jenkins was a fellow employee.

14 Morgan was Cinderford's carrier.

15 Morse was a friend of Bill's, and was his landlord when Bill worked and lodged in Gloucester.

16 William Cordwin was a newsagent, stationer, tobacconist

and seller of patent medicines. His shop was in the High Street next to that of McKuskey the tailor.

17 Ruth Price was the resident children's nurse, aged twenty, at Trafalgar House.

18 Maria Green was the daughter of Bill's landlady, aged seventeen.

19 Morgan, the carrier, delivered fish for the Brain family at Bill's lodgings in the evening, though Bill occasionally collected it himself. Bill took it to Trafalgar House the next morning.

20 George Waite was the choirmaster at the Baptist chapel, Cinderford. See Appendix.

21 On the day of the demonstration, with the agreement of the employers, all the pits in Dean closed. About four thousand colliers marched in their lodges behind bands to the Speech House, the ancient meeting-place for Foresters in the centre of the Forest. The procession was a mile long. Other trade unionists, wives and children joined them at the Speech House, swelling the numbers to between twelve and fifteen thousand. After the speeches there were games and general jollification. This was the first of many annual demonstrations or galas.

22 Timothy Mountjoy was the local miners' trade union leader. He and Brown were typical of many trade union leaders of the period in that they were strongly religious as well as advocates of trade unionism. See Appendix.

23 Brierley was the nearest village to Trafalgar.

24 Tonic sol-fa is a system for reading music. It was much used in the nineteenth century by choral societies whose members often had little formal musical training.

25 As a result of the ceaseless rain a dam in Cinderford gave way on 30 July. Men from the ironworks mended the breach and prevented serious damage by the flood.

26 Foresters in the nineteenth century, and later, would often say *evening* where we would say *afternoon*.

27 The first shift lasted from 6.00 a.m. to 2.00 p.m., the second from 4.00 p.m. to midnight.

28 Filling was shovelling coal hewn by the colliers at the coal face into trams.

29 Phonography was an early name for shorthand.

30 Superintendent H. Chip was in charge of the Cinderford police.

31 A modulator was a chart used for practising the tonic sol-fa.

32 *Police News* was a weekly newspaper that featured sensational court cases.

33 John Miller was secretary of the *Oddfellows Friendly Society* in Gloucester.

34 Bill wrote 'Preece', but the correct spelling was 'Prees'. According to the autobiography of Timothy Mountjoy, who was a contemporary of Bill's, Prees 'was a warm-hearted preacher, full of life and zeal for the Master, but he had a weak body, full of pain and suffering'. His successor, Cornelius Griffiths, who came from Merthyr Tydfil, 'was full of Welsh fire. He put his big match to the slumbering embers poor Preece had left behind, and there was a mighty blaze.' See Appendix.

35 A dipple is a slope underground.

36 This engine was one of the small steam engines that took coal along the private, narrow-gauge railway known as Brains' Tramway from the colliery to Bilson on the outskirts of Cinderford. It also pulled a 'cart' laden with colliery workers, including Bill, down to Bilson after the night shift. See picture on page 17.

37 Samuel Bennett was a friend.

38 Nathaniel and Benjamin Greening were jewellers and watchmakers in Cinderford for over a quarter of a century.

39 Dan Pogson was a colliery manager.

40 Perhaps this is a reference to the system of issuing the colliers with numbered tickets before they went down the pit so that they could come up again at the end of the shift in the same order as they descended. This was to prevent shoving and pushing at the pit bottom to get into the cage first. Alternatively it could be a reference to a more complicated system of checking who was below ground should there be an accident. Later it became generally accepted practice in pits for each collier to have

a token, which was transferred from a hook on one board in the office to a hook on another when they descended. The men at Trafalgar did not like the ticketing system. W.B.B. once defended it by saying that he had a right to know who and how many men were at work.

41 William Wood had quite a sizeable ironmonger's shop and blacksmith's in Cinderford.

42 Longs seems to have been a general shop. Among other things it sold sweets, stationery and second-hand books.

43 Wootton Hill Cottage was where Beck lived and worked.

44 Mary was Beck's fellow servant.

45 Miss Witton was Beck's employer.

46 Presumably 'Boy' was the nephew of the owner of the house.

47 C.D.V. is an abbreviation of *carte de visite*. When first introduced in 1857 this was a small card bearing a photographic likeness and was used as a visiting card. Later it meant a photograph or a picture postcard.

48 Peter Loveridge was a relation of Beck's, perhaps her brother. His wife was called Bessie.

49 By 'mails' Bill means the mail train from London.

50 'Oafed' means played the fool.

51 *Beehive* was a Labour journal, founded in 1862, which circulated mainly in London.

52 A 'love feast' was a meal in which those who had food shared with those who hadn't. The early Christians held a love-feast in conjunction with the anniversary of the Lord's Supper, when the rich provided food for the poor.

53 John Boud was a tinsmith.

54 J. Conolly was W.B.B.'s coachman.

55 Lizzie Green, aged ten, was the daughter of Bill's landlady.

56 T.W. Oakley was Bill's father.

57 Emily Cook lived in Cheltenham. She was probably there in service. Her parents lived in Cinderford. Bill later corresponded with her.

58 Highnam village is near Gloucester. Highnam church was designed by Henry Woodyer for Thomas Gambier-Parry

in 1847. The frescoes were painted by Gambier-Parry himself.

59 In addition to being a bathing place, St Anthony's Well was also a drinking fountain and a wishing well in Bill's time. Its waters, which fed the Flaxley stream and nourished the once famous Flaxley trout, also had a reputation for curing skin diseases.

60 Bill visited Miss Cook the following April.

61 Shakemantle was an iron mine a few miles away. Perhaps it was also the name given to houses nearby.

62 Oliver Green, aged fourteen, was the landlady's son.

63 The previous June four men had been killed at the Plump Hill limestone quarry, which was near Mitcheldean, when blasting involving 1½ tons of gunpowder took place. The Brains were not involved in the exercise. After the explosion the men went into the quarry before the fumes had cleared and were suffocated by them. In 1874 a more successful operation took place there, when 1 ton of gunpowder was exploded by 'Brain's patent battery'. In 1894 a bigger blast involving 4 tons of gunpowder took place. This operation was carried out by Frank Brain, chairman of the Electric Blasting Apparatus Company, and W.J. Smith with electric fuses. It displaced 36,000 tons of rock, and was witnessed by six to seven thousand people, including one from America. Three blasts from a cornet by the leader of the Drybrook Brass Band gave the signal to Smith to operate the battery. There were no casualties. See Appendix.

64 As children's nurse, Ruth Price would get up to attend to the Brain children.

65 Fossilized vegetation and tree trunks are often found in the coal strata.

66 Samuel Marling was the local Member of Parliament.

67 'Made slight boor' means he acted somewhat boorishly.

68 Maria was going to London, probably into service, and was marking her linen.

69 The tally was of the number of carts of coal brought to the surface. At the end of his diary Bill carefully copied the pit's daily tally.

70 The strange name of 'Mosooo' appears several times, with different spellings. One is Mossooooo. Its owner cannot be identified, but he seems to have been an important person at the colliery. Perhaps *Mosooo* is an anglicized version of *Monsieur* – the boss.

71 O. Williams was possibly a relation.

72 W.F. Rhodes was Cinderford's postmaster. See Appendix.

73 In fact Bill was visiting Gloucester on that day.

74 Werner was a colliery manager.

75 Bill's lodgings were at Littledean Woodside.

76 Alice was Morse's daughter, aged two.

77 The level-crossing was probably where Brain's tramway crossed the Great Western Railway line at Bilson junction.

78 Annie Kingscote, aged twenty-four, was the children's resident governess at Trafalgar House.

79 Bill uses the expression 'to do the amicable (or amiable) Quaker' several times. It was no doubt a common expression of the age. Quakers belonged to the Society of Friends, but Bill obviously had a wider concept of friendliness than the Quakers.

80 This was perhaps Emily Cook of Cheltenham.

81 Conolly was W.B.B's coachman, and apparently had some standing among the servants at Trafalgar House.

82 Thomas Frowan Rhodes, aged twenty-nine, was the son of the postmaster.

83 By 'pert' Bill means impudent.

84 Possibly Miss Witton, Beck's employer, about the 'sneerer' he wrote to Beck on 3 October.

85 'Dialling' was surveying with instruments (perhaps theodolytes).

86 The Revd Armitage died on 26 September 1872.

87 The corn was for the horses. There were about forty of them underground at Trafalgar. They were not returned to daylight until worn out, disabled or dead.

88 The Choral Union festival was the forerunner of the eisteddfods for singers, elocutionists and Forest choirs, which were held annually in Dean until 1939, often at Cinderford Baptist Chapel.

89 Thomas Phelps and Henry Morgan were being charged in court with stealing 3 tons 13 cwt of coal from Messrs Brain, and James Whitson was being charged with stealing a watch from W.B.B.

90 The Strip-and-at-it Pit was only a short distance from Trafalgar. It was owned by the Brains. The two pits were connected by a 150 yard tunnel cut through a hill, and were run in conjunction with one another. A branch of Brain's tramway went through the tunnel, transporting coal, pit props and other materials. The Trafalgar entrance to the tunnel can still be seen. This and the offices are the only parts of the colliery left.

91 Water was the bugbear of all pits, but especially in Dean. However, Trafalgar colliery was remarkably free of it.

92 This was probably Isaiah Avott, son of John and Ann Avott and the same age as Bill. Bill later moved his lodgings to the Avotts'.

93 'The telegram' was produced by some sort of internal signal system.

94 I. Morgan was a girl who lived in Cinderford.

95 Bill might well have been alarmed. Alfred Goold, also known as Captain Goold, was an important coalmaster and ironmaster in Dean. He employed about seven hundred men in his collieries and was part owner of the Soudley ironworks. He was also a magistrate, the chairman of the Westbury Union (the poor law authority that covered Cinderford) and chairman of the Forest of Dean Colliery Owners' Association.

96 By 'minutes' Bill means details.

97 The 'straight griffin' means a straight hint.

98 'Sharps' were a mixture of the coarser parts of the cereal and the finer parts of the husk.

99 'Butty' is a Forest term for friend.

100 Bill perhaps meant tapping, i.e. repairing.

101 Barling came from Newnham. He went down the pit to inspect pit horses.

102 Edwin Crawshay was a Forest coalmaster. See Appendix.

103 The announcement was to the men about the Brains'

intention to cut wages by 10 per cent. The men resented the proposal on the grounds that in the previous twelve months the price the Brains had received for coal had advanced by 100 per cent, whereas the men's wages had increased by only 30 per cent.

104 The home of Mr T.B. Brain at Drybrook, 2½ miles north of Cinderford. Euroclydon was the name of a tempestuous wind that beset St Paul on his way to Rome (*Acts 27, 14*).

105 Two pecks (dry measure) of apples would weigh about 20 lb.

106 John Brogden & Sons were industrialists in the Porthcawl and Bridgend area of South Wales. They also had an office in London. Among their many activities was building railways, and in 1872 they contracted to take part in New Zealand's first major railway construction programme. They recruited two thousand navvies in Britain to carry out the work, and sent them out, accompanied by their wives, children and equipment, in a fleet of fifteen ships.

107 This was about 20 lb of apples. A half bushel was two pecks.

108 This is perhaps 'How She Loved Me From The Second (She) Saw Me', perhaps not.

109 Leather Pit was a coal pit east of Cinderford.

110 This is possibly a reference to flooding of the railway line by the River Severn.

111 The Lilleshall Iron Company made locomotives for Trafalgar. They made the tank engine illustrated on page 17.

112 'Sprigs' were headless tapered nails.

113 Perhaps *Voltaire's* was meant.

114 The secret was perhaps that Bill was thinking of going to New Zealand with Brogdens.

115 Mrs Cook was Emily's mother.

116 The Rockey and Starkey were veins of coal and a cut-out was an underground passage.

117 The spoons were perhaps for Beck's bottom drawer.

118 Bullo was a small harbour on the River Severn a little south of Newnham. It was at the end of a railway line that ran there

from the north of the Forest via Cinderford. It was not a passenger line, being for mineral traffic only, which was why Bill rode 'with the engine'.

119 This was perhaps his father in Monmouth, or his friend Sam Farmer in Hereford, both of whom were solicitors.

120 These fuses were large-headed matches for lighting cigars and pipes in the wind.

121 Morse was a victim of the smallpox epidemic that swept Gloucester in 1872–5. The disease was especially rife in the area in which he lived because of the faulty sewers there.

122 Sellesley is 10 miles from Gloucester.

123 'Jealousy' could mean 'suspicion' in the nineteenth century.

124 'Dull' means 'slow' here.

125 Prees died eight days later.

126 Bill was now lodging with the Avotts.

127 It seems that Bill's new job at Trafalgar depended on whether or not the colliers were working.

128 Wholesalers were not buying sufficient coal to justify working a second shift.

129 Enclosures are areas in the Forest which are fenced off for the protection of the young trees growing there.

130 Griffiths seems to be his new room-mate.

131 The Good Templars was a temperance society.

Index